MEYER LEMON RICOTTA

FAVORITE MELTY MOZZARELLA

CHÈVRE FRENCH KISS

HALOUMI? HALOU-YOU!

CHIVO FRESCO

HONEYED TOAST CHEESE

FROMAGE FACILE

BROWN BUTTER BURRATA

ALE-WASHED SQUEAKIES

CURRIED PANEER

FARM-FRESH ROUNDS

TRIPLE PEPPER HACK

CHIPOTLE-LIME OAXACA

PIZZA FILATA

CLASSIC COTTAGE CHEESE

ONE-HOUR Cheese

Ricotta, mozzarella, chèvre, paneer—
even burrata. Fresh and simple cheeses
you can make in an hour or less!

CLAUDIA LUCERO

Founder of Urban Cheesecraft and Creator of DIY Cheese Kits

WORKMAN PUBLISHING, NEW YORK

Library of Congress Cataloging-in-Publication Data is available.

ISBN 978-0-7611-7748-7

Design by Sarah Smith

Photography by Matthew Benson
Food Stylist: Carrie Purcell
Prop Stylist: Sara Abalan

Author photo and process photographs copyright © Jeff Norombaba

Additional photography on pages 111, 136, 160, 216, and 221 by Lucy Schaeffer. Food Stylist: Chris Lanier. Prop Stylist: Sara Alaban.

All other photos copyright © fotolia

Workman books are available at special discounts when purchased in bulk for premiums and sales promotions as well as for fund-raising or educational use. Special editions or book excerpts also can be created to specification. For details, contact the Special Sales Director at the address below, or send an email to specialmarkets@workman.com.

Workman Publishing Company, Inc.
225 Varick Street
New York, NY 10014-4381
workman.com

WORKMAN is a registered trademark of Workman Publishing Co., Inc.

Printed in Malaysia

First printing April 2014

10 9 8 7 6 5 4

DEDICATION

For and with Jeff:
We did it, love! Now, let's get some sleep.

And to our nieces, Monique, Bianca,
and Jocelynn—the best kitchen helpers!

CONTENTS

MELTY AND GOOEY

INTRODUCTION

Cheese in one hour? you ask, *Is it really possible?* Yes, and in some cases, well under an hour. I mean it, as in ready-to-eat, fresh cheese, *really!* And though I wish I were here to blow your minds, it's not actually anything new. Our current society is not the only one that has needed to juggle busy schedules and prepare meals quickly. People have been making simple cheeses for thousands of years, and without the aid of manufactured molds, presses, and other complex equipment.

The fact that many traditional cheeses can be made easily and quickly isn't widely known, simply because many of us have lost touch with our food and its origins in general. It was not so long ago that our ancestors baked bread daily, had a pot of stock continuously simmering on the back of the stove, and regularly prepared simple dairy products like homemade butter. Making yogurt and cheese was necessary for preserving that precious milk—and its nutrients—a while longer.

It was armed with the knowledge that human beings have been making cheese for millennia, before bleach and electricity, that I taught myself to make cheese. Now I want to teach you.

MY DIY CHEESE EDUCATION

The seed was planted when I was in high school and waiting tables in an Indian restaurant in San Diego, California. I didn't work there long, but in my short tenure, I learned how to make the delicious housemade paneer. I was about seventeen years old, but already way into cooking and old-fashioned skills by that time (e.g., nine-year-old me and ten senior citizens in a macramé class). I moved on to other pursuits, but I tucked away my cheesemaking skills until many, many years later.

In 2006, my partner, Jeff, and I moved to Portland, Oregon. Fed up with a life of working very hard to afford a tiny apartment in an expensive town and never paying down student loans, we moved in search of a better life, more about quality than quantity. A reset. We wanted to buy a home with a little land to grow vegetables (I'd been reading about it in *Organic Gardening* magazine for more than five years at this point!), but until we paid off the student loans, we'd be living in an apartment. Unable to grow our own food, we signed up for a farm share of veggies.

The journey had finally begun! And oh boy, when it was time for beets and green beans,

Stretching hot curds can be therapeutic—and the resulting cheese is delicious.

we couldn't keep up. So I found information on fermented pickles, sauerkraut, and yogurt in what looked like a semidormant online homesteading magazine and I hungrily pored over the recipes. Among those were cheese recipes. My memory shot back to that first paneer, and my interest was piqued! Our chilly, rainy weather in Portland was the perfect breeding ground for my new hobby, so I couldn't wait to start, but I was a little stuck.

Recipes called for things I'd never heard of and I could not find locally: rennet, citric acid, cultures, and calcium chloride, aside from equipment like molds, butter muslin, and much more. There were several types of rennet: animal, vegetarian, liquid, tablets . . . yikes! It was more than a little overwhelming, so I started with what I could wrap my head around: hot milk and lemon juice . . . the simple beginnings of my old buddy paneer. I made paneer several times and gained some courage—it was my gateway cheese!

If the restaurant of my youth had been making their own paneer daily (a truth that previously astounded me), it started to seem reasonable that these other cheeses might be easier to make than I was assuming, as well. *Besides, cheese is an*

ancient food, I reminded myself. After an exhaustive and discouraging search for supplies and classes in Portland (this has changed drastically in more recent years), I experimented with different supplies I found online and made my first rustic cheeses.

Because I didn't want to wait a year to find out if I failed, I was very selective and focused on cheeses that did not require aging. I graduated from paneer to ricotta, mozzarella, queso blanco, and chèvre. I simplified, merged, and tweaked recipes to suit my needs. I cut recipes down to one-gallon batches, when possible. I cut out additives or steps that seemed fussy. The results were sometimes surprising (always edible), but after a little time, I learned a lot and I was regularly making unbelievably delicious cheeses! I can't explain the excitement I felt the first time I stretched mozzarella; I literally ran to Jeff to show him the melty rope of curd. We ate that entire batch of warm cheese within minutes—yep, that's about a pound and a half. You simply have never tasted anything as succulent as your own homemade warm mozzarella.

Needless to say, it was a thrill, scrumptious, and faster than baking cookies! Eureka! I felt as if I was the first person to figure this out, and I wanted to tell the world! After sharing the results of my first misshapen cheese attempts with friends and family, however, I got great feedback and interest but it was accompanied by a lot of assumptions: *Don't I need an aging cave? But I need raw milk, right? Oh no, but what about scary mold and food poisoning?* The underlying assumption seemed to be, *if it's delicious and uncommon, it must take forever and be super hard to make, right?* I was having flashbacks to my own initial doubt, and the questions came up again and again. Making simple cheese at home was clearly a lost skill.

> **"Paneer was my gateway cheese . . . [then] I graduated from paneer to ricotta, mozzarella, queso blanco, and chèvre."**

I set out to change these assumptions by teaching people how to make cheese the easy way. That's when I started my DIY cheese kit company, Urban Cheesecraft—a pursuit that led me here, writing to you in this book.

ABOUT ONE-HOUR CHEESE

If you're looking for more complex, aged cheeses (of the "stinky" variety), there are plenty of resources available, but this is not one. The recipes you'll find here are fresh, simple cheeses that look and taste (and smell) fabulous, and offer endless customization options. When you make these cheeses, you can still have energy to host "make-your-own-pizza nights" and "taco Tuesdays"—at which you will be able to share your own delicious homemade cheese! Until you share the secret, not one person will realize that you made cheese in an hour. And since I'm in the business of reclaiming lost skills, I hope you *do* share the "secret."

All of the cheesemaking techniques shared in this book are based on traditional methods: You will heat milk, add coagulant, drain, mill, salt, and press curds just like humans have done for thousands and thousands of years.

As grounded as these techniques are in cheesemaking tradition, the recipes are all fresh, modern interpretations of the classics. They came from a great deal of experimentation, which I encourage you to do as soon as you feel comfortable with the techniques. I've learned that cheesemakers are curious folks by necessity (it's a science *and* an art after all!); they've been creating and re-creating cheeses throughout history. Like them, we can invent, play, and push, because in the end, we're just helping milk live a little bit longer and delighting ourselves in the process. No need to overthink it.

Okay, if after all this, you're still with me, but bent on playing the skeptic, here's something to

Goat's milk helps nourish baby goats—and it makes amazing cheese!

prove my point: Let's just jump right in and make a small batch of cheese right now. Don't read the rest of the book. Just stop, gather some simple supplies, and follow this recipe. Continue reading once you have a snack of fresh cheese to tide you over.

WHY DIY WHEN YOU CAN BUY?

Okay, you've made First-Timer's Cheese, and have this book in your hands, so you must appreciate homemade food (or someone who gave it to you does). But just in case you don't yet realize what a

FIRST-TIMER'S CHEESE IN 5 STEPS (20 TO 30 MINUTES)

— MAKES ABOUT ½ POUND* —

INGREDIENTS & SUPPLIES

2-quart saucepan or stockpot

Slotted spoon or small mesh strainer

1-quart bowl

1 quart (4 cups) cow's milk, any type

⅛ cup vinegar (basic white, white wine, or apple cider) OR ⅛ cup lemon or lime juice

¼ teaspoon salt to taste (sea salt, flake salt, or any salt you like)

Ground pepper and/or herbs of your choice (dry or fresh will work)

1 Pour the milk into the saucepan and heat it on medium as you stir. Look for foam around the inside edges of the pot as well as little simmer bubbles coming from the bottom—not a rolling boil, but close.

2 When you see the bubbles as described, start slowly pouring in the vinegar (you may not need it all) and stir gently to incorporate it until you see the clear separation of curds (white solids) and whey (clearish liquid). The separation you see is called coagulation.

3 When you see coagulation and the liquid no longer looks like plain milk, turn the heat to low and stir the curds very, very gently as you cook them for 2 more minutes.

4 Turn off the heat and use the slotted spoon or strainer to scoop the curds into the bowl while leaving behind in the saucepan as much whey as possible. When you have all of the curds, drain any whey that has collected in the bowl.

5 Add salt and pepper (and herbs, if you like) to taste. Stir them into the curds evenly and . . .

Voilà, YOU MADE CHEESE! To be specific, you made a directly acidified farmer-style cheese. It will taste great crumbled onto salads, pizza, tacos, and chili or just eaten simply with crusty bread and ripe tomatoes.

And did you time yourself? Well under an hour. (I told you!) Congratulations—this is just the beginning.

* NOTE: Lower fat milk yields less cheese.

powerful thing it is to be the producer of your own cheese, I thought I'd list just a few good reasons.

The food we're eating now is not the food we ate a hundred or even fifty years ago. We eat antibiotics, pesticides, and additives like no other time in history. More and more people seem to be developing food sensitivities, digestive ailments, and, more recently, mysterious autoimmune disorders. And while it remains a controversial topic, I can't help but think (and much research has shown) that our food and environment are affecting our health.

Cheese, like other foods, can be mass-produced, fabricated, and made with cheap, sometimes toxic ingredients. In the plus column, manufacturing has made cheese very accessible

and affordable, but those gains have been to the detriment of our health. When you take charge of the production of your own cheese, you can choose the quality of the milk, and you may even have the opportunity to go directly to a farmer for it. You can use your own homegrown herbs or choose to purchase organic options; you can add flavor with nourishing and interesting salts rich with minerals, or leave the salt out altogether. If you wish, and this is the really fun part, you can add exciting flavors like lemon zest and cayenne pepper to create personalized palate combinations you just won't find in stores.

Moreover, if you are vegetarian, or if you can only digest goat's or raw milk, you can make a previously forbidden, wholesome treat customized just for you. As if that weren't enough, it sure doesn't get more local and environmentally friendly than making cheese in your own kitchen (unless you milk a cow in your kitchen, of course). If you have been trying to eat seasonally, and support local farmers already, you'll be happy to know that cheese can also be a part of this change. Whatever milk you purchase, when you make cheese in your own kitchen, you are the local cheesemaker. You've made one less cheese that has to be imported from another state or country.

Do-it-yourself cheese is fun to make, and it is better for you, better for your local economy and the environment, and better on your schedule, now that you can do it in less than an hour. What more do you need? Oh . . . you want it to be *yummy*, too? We're getting to that. Read on . . .

Chapter 1

PREPPING YOUR KITCHEN, YOUR PANTRY, AND YOUR MIND

THE ONE-HOUR CHEESE-MAKER'S KITCHEN

Any craft has its tools, practices, and tricks. One-hour cheese is no different—and the good news is that if I can handle the shopping and the tools and the "rules" (in general, my motto is that projects have to be fun, flexible, and easy to dive into), you can, too! In fact, some tips like keeping a herbalicious pantry are quite enjoyable. Stick to these simple guidelines and you'll be a cheesemaking fool in no time!

Cleanliness, Not Craziness

When it comes to prepping your space for making fresh cheese, the parameters are far more flexible than if you were making aged cheese. Still, it's important to start good habits now, and by following these simple practices you'll be in good shape.

1. *There's no need to make bleach a kitchen staple.* I don't use it at all. If you use the following tips, you don't need it, either. Instead, make a solution of half distilled white vinegar and half water and keep it in a spray bottle—use this as a general cleanser for your counter before you begin working. (If you don't enjoy the smell of pickles, don't worry, the vinegar smell fades as the solution dries.)

2. *Stainless steel is your friend.* Avoid using plastic or wooden utensils that can harbor bacteria in small cracks.

3. *Use fresh kitchen towels.* Your towels must be clean when you're making cheese—no grabbing the week-old dish towel (even if it smells fine, swap it out!).

4. *Use very, very hot water.* In combination with plain biodegradable soap, like Castile soap, hot water is best to wash your equipment, utensils, and molds. Avoid any detergents that might leave chemical residues. If you have a dishwasher, the hot water and steam will also get your dishes squeaky clean, but do try to buy a simple, biodegradable dishwasher soap for the same reason as noted above.

The Equipment List

The fact that our microbatch recipes use a gallon or less of milk makes it a breeze to gather these useful tools in an average kitchen—no need for five-gallon vats here! Though these are fairly common items, it's important to know why they are the chosen ones. They will be consistently used throughout the book, so this is an important read for guaranteed success.

Tight Mesh Cheesecloth
Cheesecloth is at the top of the list because it's important to note that the common cheesecloth found at most grocery stores—with huge holes—is going to ruin your (cheesemaking) life! Instead,

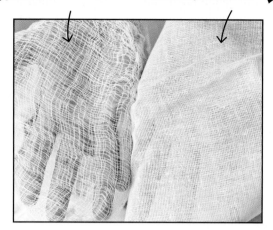

I recommend getting your hands on what is called "butter muslin" or Grade 90# (90 threads per square inch) cheesecloth. In fact, I'd rather that you use a boiled pillowcase or lint-free tea towel over the grocery-store mummy wrap. Your curds are precious, and you don't want any slipping away through the "cracks." You will need an approximately 18-inch square piece of cloth.

Thermometer

It is possible to learn to "read the milk": Plenty of people make cheese without a thermometer (lots of touching, sniffing, listening, and watching—it's pretty cool). A thermometer will be invaluable, however, while you're learning. It doesn't have to

be fancy; a 5-inch metal probe thermometer (like the kind used for meat), a simple digital version, or a food-safe glass milk thermometer (no mercury!) will do. Recipes are given in Fahrenheit (and though most thermometers give readings in °F and °C, there is a handy conversion chart on page 249). If it is analog (nondigital), look for one that:

- Includes 0°F to 220°F (-18°C to 104°C); you will be working in the range of 80°F to 200°F (27°C to 93°C).

- Shows increments of no more than 2 degrees at a time.

Those are the bare minimum requirements for a basic thermometer. Of course, you can also go deluxe and get programmable versions with alarms and other sorts of bells and whistles. They will work just fine, too. Just avoid the types with infrared beams, because the milk foam confuses them, and they give incorrect temperatures.

Microwave

One of the relatively modern tools we use to create some impressive cheeses within an hour is a microwave oven. Any size will do (in other words, the one you have in your kitchen is perfect).

We use it primarily for heating curd quickly and consistently. It is not absolutely necessary for many of the recipes—and if you don't have a microwave, I do offer an alternative hot whey method (see page 144)—but having a microwave is definitely beneficial in making several cheeses in the Melty and Gooey section (page 123). Your results will vary slightly without a microwave (the stretch won't be as apparent, for instance) and it will take a little longer to make your cheese, but the end product will still be delicious.

Stockpot

A good-sized, good quality stockpot is a core item in any kitchen, and especially useful to have when it comes to home cheesemaking. If you're blessed with a variety of options, or are thinking of investing in one, stainless-steel, glass, or enameled pots are the most ideal when it comes to cheesemaking. Whichever you choose, select a pot with the thickest base you can afford, since the thin bases have the tendency to scorch your milk (and you will have to scrub and scrub—*and scrub!*—if the pot can be saved at all). Avoid thin or old-fashioned aluminum and cast-iron pots because the acids used in the cheesemaking process can corrode the metals and give your cheese an unpleasant metallic flavor. A cast-iron *core* or aluminum *core* on an enamel-coated or nonstick pot is fine because the metals don't touch the milk and acid. As I mentioned, one large pot will cover you for the entire book, but if you have a 2- or 3-quart saucepan as well, for mini batches like Fromage Facile (page 43), it will be easier to take a temperature reading.

Colander

A large colander, mesh sieve, or strainer that can hold a gallon's worth of curds is a must: The typical size used for washing veggies is usually adequate. Stainless-steel and enameled versions are ideal, again, because of the ingredients you'll be working with (the acids in the cheesemaking process can corrode aluminum), but plastic is fine, too.

Large Bowls, Measuring Cups, and Measuring Spoons

Staples of any kitchen, a variety of bowls and measuring equipment is especially handy for the aspiring cheesemaker. For our purposes, measuring cups for liquids and solids can be used interchangeably since the difference between the two are negligible for the ratios we'll be working with.

Measuring spoons and cups made of any material will do just fine but again, to keep things easy to clean, glass cups and stainless-steel cups and spoons are great.

Sometimes, I call for heating milk or curds in the microwave, and for that use a large, microwave-safe bowl is imperative—although a large, round glass bowl or rectangular glass casserole dish will work equally well. You'll also need an extra large heat-resistant bowl (stainless steel is fine) for catching your whey. Make sure the bowl is big (deep) enough so that the curds, when placed over the bowl to drain, won't be sitting in any whey. Lastly, a large bowl, of any kind, will be handy for ice baths (see page 18, for example).

Spoons (Slotted/Plain) and Whisks

Certain mixing utensils will become your favorites, but it's nice to have a variety to work with from the get-go. Of all the utensils you see above, I use the small slotted spoon and the whisk most frequently. Ultimately, the determining factors in selecting utensils are 1) the size of your hands and what's comfortable in them, and 2) the type of cheese you're making and the actions the recipe calls for (stirring, cutting, or scooping curds). Stainless steel is best (as I've noted throughout), but you can use bamboo, wood, or plastic in a pinch (scrub them well!).

Molds

Professional cheese molds (basically, white cups with little holes or slits) are neat—and we'll get into this in more detail—but once you start making and molding your cheese, you're going to start looking at the items in your cupboards in a very different way: in terms of cheese shapes. Maybe that yogurt cup you had at breakfast makes a nice onetime mold—you could poke holes into it or leave it as is depending on how much moisture you want to leave in your cheese. What about your cupcake or

CUPCAKE TINS MAKE CUTE LITTLE CHEESE WHEELS!

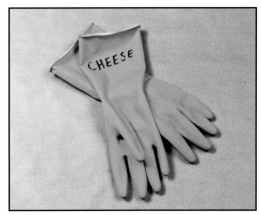

tart pans? Silicone ice trays? Cookie cutters, sushi rice molds, coffee cups, small bowls, ramekins, loaf pans, and measuring cups all make great molds. Any sort of food-safe container, really, is fair game. Parchment or waxed paper can be part of the process, too, whether you line a mold for easy extraction and added texture; use it to ball, roll, or twist your cheese into shape; or simply use a sheet as a smooth, clean surface to work on. Turn to page 184 for a full tour of cheese molds and shapers.

Gloves

Though your clean, bare hands work just fine, rubber gloves are also helpful for keeping your cheese pristine while you work. More often, however, gloves may be called upon to protect your hands from hot whey while shaping or straining. The more cheese you make, the more your fingers will get used to it, and the easier it will be to gauge whether or not you feel up to plunging your bare mitts into the hot whey. Tip: Take a permanent marker and write *"cheese"* on the wrists of your gloves so they don't inadvertently get used to scrub the tub!

Maintenance

To keep things simple, follow these tips for maintaining your supplies and keeping your equipment in good, working order.

1. For any equipment that will come in contact with milk (a pot, spoon, and so on), place it in a large bowl of cold water as you finish using it. Then wash it in very hot, soapy water (see notes on recommended soaps, page 7).

2. The cheesecloth can be reused again and again if you drop it in cold water immediately after use, then rinse the curds off. After you're done cleaning up, either wash it completely by hand with hot water and soap *or* rinse it very well, then hang it to dry, and fully wash it with your kitchen laundry in the next load.

3. If you have some curds sticking at the bottom of a stainless-steel pot, sprinkle in some regular flake salt and scrub at it with a sponge. This has worked better for me than any specialized scrubbers.

THE ONE-HOUR CHEESEMAKER'S PANTRY

The following ingredients are all you'll need to make any of the cheeses in this book—and more! You can stock your pantry as you go or all at once. Most items are nonperishable and keeping them on hand will allow you to make cheese when the inspiration (or craving) strikes!

The Basic Ingredients

ACIDS

Acids are key to the one-hour cheesemaker's pantry because they trigger the first step in transforming milk into cheese. It's helpful to have a variety on hand, but they will also accumulate naturally as you try the recipes that call for each of them. I'm also willing to bet that you already have one or more of these at home.

Vinegars White wine vinegar, apple cider vinegar (raw or not), and distilled white vinegar are all on my shelf. And you can experiment with others. It's important to note, however, that every vinegar varies slightly in acidity—and each will subtly contribute to the flavor of your cheese. Some may be more enjoyable to you than others, but if you ever find the flavor too strong, rinse the curds with tepid water while draining them.

Citrus Fresh and bottled lemon juice and lime juice are the basics, though you may enjoy playing with more unexpected citrus options like kumquats,

calamansi, or Meyer lemons (Meyer Lemon Ricotta, page 35). Like vinegar, each citrus fruit varies in acidity and will impart its own flavor to the cheese.

Citric Acid A weak acid compound and natural preservative found in lemons, limes, and other citrus fruits, citric acid is sold in salt form and appears white and granulated. (It is also sometimes labeled "sour salt" and is, interestingly, what is used to coat sour gummy candies.) Your grocery store may carry it in the bulk or canning section, or turn to the Resources, page 248, for other places to find it.

SALTS

While salt may seem to be a surprisingly nuanced ingredient, sodium content and other factors (like additives) can range from type to type.

Fine and Flaky Salt First and foremost, I recommend pure salts—kosher-style flake salt or cheese salt—for general flavoring, since they dissolve easily into the curds. Fine pickling salt or standard sea salt can also work, but you must reduce the amount called for in the recipe by about a quarter (and then adjust to taste when your cheese is in the drained curd stage) since equal amounts of finely granulated salts have a much higher ratio of salt to volume.

Read the labels and make sure that there aren't any anticaking agents included in your salt. You'd be surprised what you can find on an ingredients label!

Textured Salts Finishing salts that add crunch, color, or special flavor to one of your homemade cheeses can be any texture that you enjoy, since they don't have to dissolve.

RENNET

A compound of enzymes that can be derived from animal, vegetable, or microbial sources, rennet is used to help out with cheese's coagulation process.

Vegetarian Rennet Tablets I use vegetarian rennet tablets exclusively in these recipes. They're easy to portion out, they store well (keep them in the freezer!), and as the name implies, vegetarians can eat the resulting cheese! It's now very easy to get these online (see Resources, page 248), and maybe even in your local stores (look for cheesemaking supplies). The brands I use are Danisco, Marshall, or Fromase.

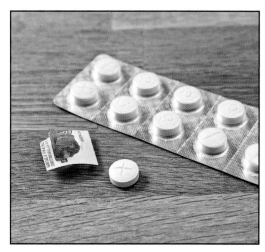

Animal Rennet Tablets or Liquid Rennet

You may come across tablets made with animal ingredients, as well as liquid varieties of rennet. I do encourage you to look for and use the recommended vegetarian tablets for sure success with these recipes. Measurements for all rennet options vary, so substitutions will not be obvious. Avoid the animal rennet tablets found in the gelatin section of grocery stores. They are intended for custard and though you can use them to make some cheeses, they are weak and not appropriate for these recipes.

TIP! An inexpensive pill cutter is great for splitting rennet tablets. They're available at most pharmacies.

HERBS AND SPICES

Keep a diverse collection of dry herbs and spices on hand to customize the taste of your cheese. Some great core basics are black pepper, chili flakes, smoked paprika, dill, chives, thyme, and mixed Italian herbs. The more you stock, the more you can experiment with the flavor and look of your cheeses. Many spice brands now make additive-free blends so you can create complex flavor more easily (rainbow peppercorns, lemon garlic pepper, and a Mexican chili blend are just a couple of my faves). Buy fresh herbs with the seasons or, better yet, grow your own! Get some starts and some seeds and see if you can grow yourself a cheese herb garden. Before I had a yard, I grew a pot of garlic chives indoors. You just stick a couple of cloves of store-bought garlic in a pot of soil, blunt side down, and keep them moist. They will sprout little green chives from the pointy tip in a few days. You will have flavorful garlic chives to snip in no time—any time of year!

MILK

Not all milk is created equal. Here are the two most important things to remember when choosing milk to make your cheese:

1. The less your milk has been altered since the time of milking, the easier your cheesemaking experience will be. (The least altered milk is raw milk.)

2. The closer the milk was produced to your home, the better, because it has likely not been processed for long travel and storage. Read labels for origin.

Don't happen to have a cow in the backyard? No worries—not many of us do! Every recipe in this book can be made with plain, store-bought, pasteurized milk (as long as it's not *ultra-pasteurized,* you're set).

Although every brand of milk I have tested has worked, some make the coagulation process easier (sturdy curd, easy stretch, for example) and the final cheeses are closer to the ideal artisanal results the first time you try making them.

In each cheese recipe, I've indicated the recommended milk (fat content, cow or goat, and so on) for a recipe, but the recipes are flexible, and substitutions are easy. Read on for tips on finding the milk that will work for you. You may run into these different labels when you start paying more attention to your milk.

Ultra-Pasteurized Milk This form of milk has been heated at a higher temperature than pasteurized milk—usually under pressure at 280°F for two seconds. In a pinch, it can be used to make a loose, acid-coagulated cheese like Meyer Lemon Ricotta, but it cannot be used to make the cheeses that contain rennet (like Favorite Melty Mozzarella or Pizza Filata). Though regular pasteurization is enough to make "sick" milk safer, ultra-pasteurization extends the shelf life of milk from eighteen days to up to sixty days. In the cheesemaking process, ultra-pasteurization can result in a loose curd because all good bacteria are killed along with the bad, and the milk's protein and calcium have been weakened. If you find yourself with mozzarella that wants to flop into ricotta, ultra-pasteurized milk is likely the problem. The labeling is not always clear and does not have to appear front and center: Look everywhere on the jug to find UP, UHP, or Ultra-Pasteurized and then steer clear.

Organic Milk Buying organic is generally the best choice when choosing our food, but don't assume that all organic milk brands are good for making cheese. Unfortunately, even organic brands practice ultra-heat pasteurization, so that their milk can travel great distances and have a long shelf life, too. As mentioned above, ultra-heat pasteurization alters the structure of the milk and we do need some nature to work with. Look beyond the

"Organic" label and do not stop at a "Natural" label, which is not regulated at all.

Pastured Milk Not to be confused with pasteurized milk, pastured means that the cows providing the milk get to eat grass (as opposed to the soy and corn that a lot of commercial livestock is fed). You're lucky if you can find this, because aside from independent farms, only one larger dairy is currently marketing "grass milk" among their offerings.

A NOTE ABOUT RAW MILK

Children, infants, and women who are pregnant or nursing are advised by the American Academy of Pediatrics against consuming raw or unpasteurized milk products because they may harbor harmful bacteria. If this describes you, consult a doctor before consuming raw milks or cheeses.

Raw or Unpasteurized Milk This unprocessed milk transforms into cheese most easily, and is my favorite to work with because the live bacteria, enzymes, and intact proteins and calcium all assist with rennet activity and coagulation, but it's important to educate yourself about the risks of using raw milk, and to find a reputable source for your raw milk. A farm, for instance, will not necessarily provide better milk than a grocery store if the farm engages in unsanitary milking practices or the milk or animals are kept in unhealthy conditions. You may live in a state where raw milk sales are legal in grocery stores, but if you do not, you can purchase straight from a small farm legally (click your state in the finder on realmilk.com to find milk near you).

Pasteurized, Unhomogenized Milk In my cheesemaker's wonderland, safe raw milk is available for everyone, but the other milk I would like to have readily available for all in every grocery store is *unhomogenized,* or cream line, milk. As with raw milk, the cream separates to the top of the bottle, making a clear line between it and the milk. The only difference between this milk and raw milk is that it has been pasteurized, usually only lightly. Look to see if your grocery store carries this milk!

Pasteurized, Homogenized Milk This milk is the easiest to find in most grocery stores. Pasteurized milk has generally been heated at 167°F for fifteen seconds. This kills pathogenic bacteria that may have made it into the milk, but unfortunately, it also alters the friendly bacteria and enzymes that make it easier for rennet to cause coagulation in milk. I do give you instructions on how to lightly pasteurize raw milk (page 24) if you'd like to take care of it yourself. You will not see the cream line mentioned above in homogenized milk because the fat has been mixed evenly into the milk.

Cultured Buttermilk Commonly found in the dairy section of most grocery stores (right next to the regular milk!), cultured buttermilk is actually low-fat cow's milk with cultures added. If you've tasted it, you know that it is tangy and acidic—a little like sour cream. These qualities are why it's called for in Fromage Facile (page 43), Classic Cottage Cheese (page 57), and other recipes. Cultured buttermilk is different than the fresh buttermilk you will create as

a byproduct when you make Butter (page 236). *Fresh* buttermilk can be used in bread, biscuit, and pancake recipes as well as simple smoothies. It is delicious and mild in flavor but it is not tangy nor cultured.

Cream Cream is simply the fat that will separate from fresh, unhomogenized milk (or that is mixed into homogenized milk). It may also bear the label Heavy Cream or Heavy Whipping Cream (and, if you can't find another, even Light Whipping Cream will work in our recipes, all unsweetened and without gums or other additives). You can find it raw in some states, pasteurized and ultra-pasteurized in all others. Try to find it raw or just plain pasteurized but if you can't, ultra-pasteurized will still add the richness we're looking for in recipe like Brown Butter Burrata (page 171).

Though I encourage you to buy the best milk you can afford and find, it's also wise to experiment with a gallon of an easy-to-find milk—because if it makes a good cheese, you know you can grab it at the last minute if needed.

The better the milk, the better the cheese!

The Basic Science (and the Magic) of One-Hour Cheese

If you're the analytical type, and don't just want to make cheese (and eat it!), but are interested in knowing what's *happening*, here's the deal on these fresh cheeses in a nutshell. I've intentionally kept the science at Level 1 so I don't scare anyone off, but if you'd like more information, there is a list of helpful, more advanced books in the Resources (page 248) that will contain details pertaining to aged cheeses. In the meantime, these are the major players and the parts they play in the basic cheesemaking equation.

FUNCTIONS OF THE KEY INGREDIENTS

Milk

Milk, the anchor of all cheesemaking processes, is made up of water, fats, proteins, bacteria, a sugar called lactose, minerals, and more. If milk has not been pasteurized, it also contains lactase, the enzyme that helps you digest it.

Acid

When you add an acid to hot milk, the result can be called curdling, gelling, clotting, separation, and/or coagulation. I most often use the term coagulation. In order to make cheese in one hour, I like to acidify the milk with vinegars and citrus juices. In some cases, I leave it at that because the acid alone will produce the texture I'm after (crumbly Chivo Fresco, for example, page 75). In other cases, the acid assists the rennet and they will work together to give a completely different result (Favorite Melty Mozzarella, page 137).

By adding vinegar or citrus juice, we mimic the acidification that occurs spontaneously—to some extent—if you let fresh raw milk sit at room temperature for several hours. The naturally occurring friendly bacteria within the milk eat the sugar (lactose) and produce lactic acid. It is this acid that also imparts a tart, yogurtlike cultured flavor and causes a separation between curds and whey. It's almost as if milk cannot help but become cheese. (Of course, somewhere along the line, human beings observed its tendency to acidify and curdle, and figured out several brilliant ways in which to manipulate that process to our delicious advantage.)

SUGARS END IN -OSE; ENZYMES END IN -ASE.

Rennet

Rennet, whether vegetarian or animal-based, contains enzymes that modify proteins in milk. In the tradition of utilizing every part of a valuable animal used for food, rennet has historically been derived from the stomach of an unweaned ruminant animal—a kid (a goat!) or calf, for example—whose digestive system is equipped with the enzymes necessary to hold and ferment its mother's milk before assimilating it further. To explain how the heck this was discovered, there is a legend that starts with a nomad carrying milk in a pouch made of a calf's stomach lining. With time and the right temperature, the milk fermented. Not wanting to waste precious milk, the nomad tasted the chunky milk, enjoyed it, and lived to tell the tale. Over time, this led us to more experimentation, resulting in a wide array of dairy delicacies that we consume today.

That predigestion that the calf's stomach enzymes (the most plentiful being chymosin or rennin) provides is what changes the structure of proteins in milk for cheesemaking. Animal rennet comes in liquid form most often (stomach lining tincture, essentially), although some less potent tablets do exist. Much to the delight of vegetarians and squeamish folk, it is also possible to coagulate milk with plant-based enzymes made from thistles (specifically cardoon stamens), a Mexican berry called trompillo, and even fig juice, among others. Since these can give unpredictable results, vegetarian rennet is also manufactured and comes in liquid or tablet form. As I've mentioned, I use vegetarian rennet tablets most often and all of the fresh cheese recipes in this book that call for rennet call for these tablets exclusively (see Resources, page 248). The enzymes (primarily *Rhizomucor miehei*) in vegetarian rennet are derived from the fungi family.

Vegetarian rennet tablets provide many conveniences that really work for our purposes. Unlike animal rennet, or even liquid vegetarian rennet, vegetarian rennet tablets are very shelf stable—and can last years if kept in the freezer! It is easy to measure and cut and use by the quarter (usually a quarter per gallon of milk) because the tablets are scored—a pill cutter is a great tool, and inexpensive. Some say that aged cheese can taste bitter when made with these tablets, but that's not a concern with one-hour cheese!

Salt

Salting the curds is another important transformative process in the making of cheese. It not only flavors the cheese pleasingly, but draws out moisture, which is important in creating the right texture and density. Salt is also a great preservative and, under the right conditions, can help turn a previously highly perishable substance (milk) into a stable cheese that doesn't require regular refrigeration. When making one-hour cheese, we only use salt for flavor and to control the amount of whey we leave in the curds for texture.

IMPORTANT FACTORS

The following are not complicated processes (no doubt you have used them for other kitchen purposes), but it does help to understand what roles the different actions play in cheesemaking, whether you're troubleshooting, adjusting textures, or even creating your own cheese recipes.

Heat

Heat helps accomplish many important steps when making cheese. It helps the enzymes in the rennet transform the milk proteins for coagulation; it shrinks curds so that they can withstand kneading and stretching (as with Chipotle-Lime Oaxaca, page 161). And it aids in refining the texture of the cheese (like helping achieve the chewy factor in the Ale-Washed Squeakies, page 113).

Ice Baths

Ice baths and washes help to cool warm curd quickly. In general, this helps the fats seize up so that there is little to no further expansion. An ice bath keeps the cheese ropes rounded (not flattened by their own warmth) when making Pizza Filata string cheese (page 151). It also secures that characteristic curd-in-cream look and feel with the Classic Cottage Cheese (page 57), which, without the ice bath, would resemble more closely a creamy and uniform ricotta.

Pressure

Cheeses like Curried Paneer (page 67) and Chivo Fresco (page 75) benefit from a little pressing because they are intended to be dense cheeses. The warm, lumpy curds are fused together with the help of some pressure to make the texture more uniform. As the curd cools, the cheeses firm up, making them easier to cut and cook.

THE ONE-HOUR
CHEESEMAKER'S MIND

There is a general mystique surrounding the cheesemaking process—and some people fear that seeming unknown. But try to set that aside, and take on a playful attitude as you allow yourself time to learn. I've included some helpful information and techniques in this section (that I wish I'd had when I was learning) to put your mind at ease before and after you make your first cheeses.

The First of
Many Pep Talks

If you've already conquered the cheese challenge on page 4, then you've already had a taste (ha!) of victory! Making cheese can be thrilling once you get going, but if you have trouble getting started or bouncing back after a surprising result—dry ricotta or rubbery mozzarella?—refer to this section. Each of the recipes in this book is designed to be incredibly user-friendly, but making cheese is still a craft and all crafts require practice.

Even if you follow the step-by-step photos to a T, your first results may not be what you expected. The good news is that your cheese is probably still madly delicious and only a slight tweak is required for next time.

The fact is, the difference between one cheese and another can be a simple ingredient change or a five-degree temperature variance—and rest

assured that even professional cheesemakers run into this issue . . . *all the time!* If you stumble across an unfamiliar result (whether related to texture or flavor), it's likely you have still created some kind of cheese, but have unwittingly discovered a new recipe not included in this book! You'll find yourself in uncharted territory—and a true DIY cheese pioneer. It is not uncommon for professional cheesemakers to discover their most popular cheese by mistake. You should be proud and not at all discouraged or hard on yourself. Just turn to my Smoky Cheater recipe (page 103) for my best "mistake" to date.

So please, before throwing your slotted spoon in the air and deciding that cheesemaking is not for you, come by for a pep talk and refer to the Troubleshooting section (page 25) to find out what the likely issue is and how to adjust for it next time. Press on, my cheese-loving friend! You'll get there.

Tricks of the Trade
(to Have Up Your Sleeve)

Here are some tips and tricks I've learned over the years through extensive research as well as plenty of trial and error. As you practice, you will find tricks, so consider yourself an expert if you discover your own exciting new methods that suit you perfectly.

HEATING MILK: TO DOUBLE BOIL OR NOT TO DOUBLE BOIL?

You may come across cheesemaking recipes online or in other books that instruct you to use a double boiler exclusively to heat the milk since it does so gently and slowly. Heating milk directly in the pot can be challenging when you're working at high temperatures, but my recipes don't call for double boiling because I believe that by following these three tips, you can heat milk successfully *and* save time.

1. Let the milk get to room temperature. If you know you will be making cheese later, leave the milk out for an hour or two. Those thirty degrees or so will save you time and sticky pots when you're heating the milk to almost boiling.

2. Use the heaviest-bottomed pot you have or consider investing in one. The milk sugars will be less likely to burn and stick to the bottom because heat is absorbed and dispersed more evenly. You can also use a nonstick pot.

3. Start out with medium heat and decrease or increase it as you judge the progress of the milk. When you stir, monitor the bottom of the pot with a spoon to check for any sticking milk. Since milk is full of lactose (a sugar, remember?), it wants to stick and brown (caramelize). Adjust the heat, stir, and don't walk away. You want to avoid a burned flavor in your milk as well as a scorched mess. You may still see some milk sticking, but if it is white and easily removed when you stir, that is perfectly fine.

DIY DOUBLE BOILER

If you do decide that you want to gently heat the milk, here's how to create a double boiler from items you may already have in your kitchen: Fill a large pot (any kind is okay, because your milk and acid will not come into contact with it) about one third of the way with water, then rest a heat-safe, nonreactive bowl (a stainless-steel or thick glass mixing bowl) or smaller pot containing the milk inside the larger pot, on top of the simmering water. Be careful not to overflow the water pot!

You still have to monitor the heat in order to get the temperature you want, but there is little risk of scorching or overheating now (though it will easily add fifteen to twenty minutes to your process when you heat a gallon of milk). This is a very helpful technique to use when you graduate

to more sensitive and complex cheeses that require aging. But, since none of the recipes here are aged, if you can avoid a double boiler, you will be rewarded with speed!

DRAINING CURDS: SO MANY WAYS, SO LITTLE TIME

Here are two methods I like to employ in the kitchen when I'm making cheese. The cloth-lined colander is an old standby, and the hanging cheese bag comes in handy when you're anxious to speed up the draining process.

Draining Method 1: Cloth-Lined Colander

Unless you are in a huge hurry, this type of draining will be sufficient for the cheese recipes in this book. If you're relatively inexperienced in the kitchen, or just charmingly accident-prone, here are two tips to keep in mind when you drain this way:

1. Place a big bowl under your cloth-lined colander even if you don't plan on reserving the whey. It's just a little insurance in case you get distracted at some point and can't remember if you actually added the citric acid, or if you were hoping that the grocery store cheesecloth with huge gaping holes would catch your curds and you find yourself with a "less-than-ideal situation." The bowl will catch anything that comes through the colander and you will still have a chance to try to adjust things without having lost your curds down the drain.

2. Cheesecloth can shrink a little and end up quite wrinkly after it's been dried in a clothes dryer. To make it smooth and flat again, wet it and wring it out thoroughly before lining your colander. This will make your cloth stretch out and cling to the colander so that your flowing curds and whey don't shift it, causing your precious curds to slide under the cloth and down the drain. It's messy and sad, and may leave you cursing like a sailor.

I usually opt for this passive colander technique over the hanging cheese bag (Method 2, next page), but it can result in a slower drain if you're dealing with a small creamy curd like that in Meyer Lemon Ricotta (page 35) or Chèvre French Kisses (page 49). Depending on your curds, cloth, and colander, a seal can occur between the hot saturated cloth and the colander, or the tiny curds can clog the small holes, and either literally stop drainage or slow it to a trickle. I like to keep an eye on the process and help it along by stirring, lifting the cloth every few minutes, or rocking it back and forth if I need to, to unclog the cloth.

Draining Method 2: Hanging Cheese Bag

Cheesemakers are inventive folks. If you look online, you can read about people hanging their curds on bungee cords, over the bathtub, on tripods, and all kinds of other creative contraptions. It is true that sometimes the fastest way to drain whey (out of small curds especially) is to create a cheesecloth bundle and hang it. Which will also have the effect of making your kitchen look like a charming pioneer homestead. It's very simple to create and hang your "bag" like the pros.

1. Line a colander with cheesecloth, pour or spoon your curds and whey into the cloth, and when you can, safely (careful, hot whey!), grab the corners of the cloth and tie them into a loose knot. Now, you can do a couple of things. . . .

2a. Put a spoon through the knot's hole and hang the bag in a tall vessel like the rinsed milk pot or a tall pitcher to catch the whey, as shown.

b. Or tie the bag from a place in your kitchen where it will not be in your way: Most people use their cupboard handles and knobs or the kitchen sink's faucet. Use cotton string to lengthen the bundle if the cloth ends are not very long. Whey is full of lactose, so your cupboards will get sticky if the wet cheesecloth is resting on them.

Though all of these hanging methods work, you'll need to experiment to see what works best for you. I always seem to be doing other things in the kitchen while I'm making cheese and I end up needing to use the sink or needing access to that particular cupboard, so I am very happy that I accidentally

MY PORTABLE CURD BAG HANGER

My own personal curd bag hanger is . . . a banana tree! I picked one up at a thrift store and discovered that it's amazing for draining curds. I just hang my bag on the hook and place the banana tree in a bowl to catch the whey—and I can put it anywhere! You can even stow it away in a cold oven or in a different room, if you happen to have curious cats. The point is, it's portable!

DIY PRESS: MAKE A "FANCY" PRESS IN ONE MINUTE

One of the really great time- and effort-saving features of these simple recipes is that very little to no pressing is required. Pressing is needed in aged cheeses to keep a consistent curd that will hold up to the aging process for months. The little pressing for the recipes in this book is nothing like the twenty-four-hour-plus processes that require pressing at ten pounds for three hours followed by twenty pounds for eight hours, then thirty-five pounds for twelve hours, and so on. For our purposes, the most convenient fresh cheese press to fashion is a water-filled milk jug. It's handy, and you can alter the weight by changing the amount of water in the jug or carton. Just be sure to place a flat item (plate or lid) on your cheese wheel first, then put the gallon on top, as shown.

For smaller containers, you can use glass jars and bottles filled with water, decorative marbles, or river pebbles—even a can of beans works in a pinch! Strong rubber bands around the whole deal can create more pressure if you need it. But note, you should only see clear whey drain out of mold holes; no milky stuff or you could be losing precious fat.

Water-filled gallon jug = DIY cheese press!

A jar or bottle works for smaller batches.

came upon my own ideal method (see "My Portable Curd Bag Hanger," opposite page). Note: All cheesemakers think their method is best!

STORING, SHARING, FREEZING

As fancier and fresher cheeses become more widely available in grocery stores, we are collectively becoming more familiar with delicacies such as fresh mozzarella and feta stored in whey and brine. They look lovely, but please note that none of the cheeses in this book should be stored in water or whey. A glass container with a lid is ideal for storing your cheeses, but you may also use plastic containers, zip-top sandwich bags, and so on.

Most of the cheeses in this book will freeze semisatisfactorily if the alternative is wasting them. (But come on, wouldn't your coworker or neighbor be delighted to receive the gift of cheese?) The texture of the melty cheeses like mozzarella is best fresh (like, that same evening), but if you need to freeze some you can do so in an airtight container and use it within a month. You will definitely note some difference in texture and creaminess, but the cheeses are still great for cooking, crumbling, or shredding after they've been thawed.

HOW TO DECHLORINATE WATER

Some of my recipes call for dechlorinated water because chlorine can inhibit rennet activity. Please don't get me wrong, I'm not requiring nor encouraging you to buy bottled water. If you have it, you can use filtered water from your fridge dispenser, your sink faucet, or a special pitcher. If you don't have filtered water, leave an open jar of tap water on your counter for eight to twenty-four hours and enough of the chlorine will evaporate for the purposes of these recipes (nicer for drinking, too). As an alternative, blend a cup of water in your blender for a couple of minutes (really!) to let the water breathe a bit. I use straight tap water where I live in Portland, Oregon, so you can also just go for it if you don't notice a strong swimming pool smell in your tap water. If you don't get clear coagulation, however, chlorine may be an issue.

HOW TO LIGHTLY PASTEURIZE RAW MILK

If you just aren't sure about raw milk yet (see page 15), you can use this at-home method to lightly pasteurize it yourself. The properties the milk retains will still allow you to get a good curd at cheesemaking time and result in some really great cheese (the milk will be lightly pasteurized, but not homogenized—and that helps).

1. Pour the raw milk into a pot or double boiler (see page 20 for more on double boiling).

2. Heat the milk to 145°F, stirring every couple of minutes. Stay close to make sure it does not accidentally boil.

3. Hold the temperature at 145°F for exactly 30 minutes. Closely monitor it: You may need to increase and decrease the heat to stay at this temperature.

4. Turn off the heat and place the pot in the sink or in a larger pot filled with ice water. Stir constantly until the temperature drops to 40°F.

Congratulations. Your milk has been lightly pasteurized, and now you can use that milk to make some amazing cheese!

Curd Support (aka Troubleshooting Basics)

Most how-to books have the troubleshooting section *after* the instructions, but as a teacher, I like my students to feel proactive in the classroom. If you read through these troubleshooting tips *before* hitting the kitchen, you may even recognize where you need to make an adjustment as you go. But please try not to get hung up on them. As it goes when riding a bike, keep your eye on where you want to go, not where you might fall.

Aside from the notes below, I've included additional tips specific to each cheese throughout the recipes, but the bottom line is: Try the finished cheese, even if it looks different than you expected. It may be simply delicious, and just waiting to be paired with cracked pepper, olive oil, and bread. But don't worry, we'll still get to the bottom of this, so your cheese will be even better next time!

PROBLEM: My Meyer Lemon Ricotta, French Kisses, and other creamy cheeses are crumbly and dry.

This is the most common rookie issue so let's really dig into it. Okay, this is our checklist:

☐ **Did you follow the recipe exactly? Retrace your steps. I know you were excited to eat cheese!**

☐ **Did you use the recommended milk and acid?**

☐ **Did you heat the milk for the specified amount of time at the given temperature?**

Following the Recipe Making cheese in one hour or less is awesome, but these recipes are not passive and do require your attention for the full time. So block out the time and proceed with care. Read every recipe all the way through first and gather your supplies, taking care to double-check measurements and temperatures. This "practice run" and familiarity will often prevent a quick grab for the wrong measuring spoon. . . . Adding twice as much citric acid can make a huge difference in your cheese!

Fat Not enough fat can make these cheeses crumbly and/or rubbery. The texture and mouthfeel of your cheese is not going to be quite right unless you use the recommended milk (i.e., if the recipe calls for whole milk but you use nonfat milk, the cheese will be dry), but you can leave a bit more moisture in a cheese like Meyer Lemon Ricotta or Fromage Facile by draining it less (leaving more whey in it).

Acid Too much acid can make cheeses tough. All vinegars vary in acidity, and lemons and limes in particular can vary from one fruit to the next, but it's easy to learn how to work with them. Next time, try cutting the acid by ½ teaspoon. You will know if you cut it too much if the whey still looks a lot like milk (that's potential cheese you're leaving behind!) and you end up with a lot less cheese than the recipe says you will. So reduce the acid just a little. If you suspect you cut too much, you can probably still stir it in.

Temperature Pay careful attention to the temperatures called for in the recipes. Insert the thermometer into different parts of the pot after stirring (when possible) to avoid hot or cool spots and monitor frequently. Realize that if your milk suddenly jumped up in temperature (did you check your email?) or if you left it to heat for longer than directed, the result will change and your cheese may be crumbly and dry (but don't throw it out—you can press most crumbly results into a paneerlike cheese).

☐ **Is your thermometer accurate? (See the box at the right to check.)**

Thermometers can be "shocked" out of calibration with extreme temperatures or rough handling. If your thermometer is not reading accurately, it is possible that you could overheat your milk, resulting in a tough and dry curd, or that you could underheat it, resulting in a loose curd, one that never coagulates or won't stretch when it should.

☐ **You followed the recipe, and your thermometer is correct; is it possible that the curd was exposed to too much heat and too much air?**

Simple things like how long you marveled at your beautiful curds as you stirred in the salt can change the texture of your cheese.

Salt and Air As you stir the curd, it releases moisture, especially with the aid of salt. You are also exposing the curd to air, which serves as a drying agent, as well. The most tender ricotta, for example, demands very little stirring and minimal exposure to air.

Heat As mentioned earlier, curd can toughen if it is allowed to sit in hot whey for a longer time than recommended. Heat encourages the curd to release water (in the form of whey), causing the curd to shrink. These are good properties to know, since you can use this knowledge for good should you ever want to adjust your results or create your own recipes. With creamy cheeses, however, we want to drain, stir, and air curds out as little as possible. Stop stirring and draining the curds as soon as you see a cheese texture that you like. If you see the curd change from spreadable to crumbly, well, you went a little too far, but now you know for next time. It should only take one

CHECK AND RECALIBRATE YOUR THERMOMETER

Though the point of having a thermometer is to achieve a certain degree (ha!) of precision, sometimes even the fanciest of instruments can get out of whack. To find out if yours is still providing an accurate reading, follow these steps:

1. Fill a cup with ice and pour just enough water in to cover the ice. Stir.

2. Remove any case or cover on your thermometer.

3. Dip 3 inches (or whatever the manufacturer instructs) of the thermometer into the icy water for about 30 seconds. The temperature should read very close to freezing temperature 32°F (to 35°F would be okay).

4. If it differs by more than 5 degrees, and if your thermometer allows you to adjust the reading, do so until it reads the correct temperature. If it does not, purchase a new thermometer.

or two times before you get to know how each process can and should go in order to achieve the ideal result you're after. There may still be some variety in your results, but this is what we call the handmade charm, right?

PROBLEM: I never, ever get coagulation and/or I can't ever stretch the stretchy cheeses.

Coagulation If you know that you followed the recipe, acidified as directed, and have the proper rennet, the quality of your milk is likely to blame. You will either need to try a different brand or add calcium chloride to the milk you have to repair the milk's structure a little. See Resources (page 248) to purchase it, and then add ¼ teaspoon mixed into ¼ cup of water as soon as you add the milk to the pot.

Stretching Using a microwave makes heating and stretching this type of cheese easier. If you opt to use the hot whey method (see page 144), you will likely not be able to stretch the curd as it appears in the photos. If the curd feels bouncy, you're on the right track! Just fold, press, or roll the curd into a shape that resembles that in the photos as closely as possible. If you did use a microwave and you are not achieving an impressive stretch, try heating the curds for another thirty seconds to adjust for your microwave—or knead them ten more times to encourage the transformation from a blob of lumpy curds into a springy ball of bouncy cheese.

PROBLEM: My Favorite Melty Mozzarella and Chipotle-Lime Oaxaca are waxy-looking and hard as rocks.

If you're using the right milk and did not add extra rennet, then the curd got too hot at some point. It could have happened 1) during the initial heating just before or just after you added the rennet, or 2) later, when you heated it for stretching.

Reading Temperature It's possible that your pot of warming milk is not all a uniform temperature. Your burner could burn hotter in some spots than others. To get an accurate reading, stir right before

a temperature reading so that you incorporate milk from the outer edges with the middle and everything in between. Even after that, take the temperature in two different places in the pot, to be sure. Otherwise, it's possible that you think the milk is only 100°F, when it is actually 120°F—which will change your results dramatically.

Heating for Stretching It is also possible to overheat the curd, whether you use a microwave or a hot whey bath. Pouring boiling whey over your mozzarella curd will turn it into a rubber ball in a hurry. Similarly, extra time in the microwave along with a lot of extra stretching can also make your cheese waxy and tough. It is a combination of overheating and releasing too much whey and butter fat that can create rubbery cheese. Stick to the temperatures and instructions given in a recipe; they *are* important.

> "Use this knowledge for good: Adjust your results or create your own recipes."

The takeaway: You may encounter surprising results, but you should be able to prevent them by reading a recipe all the way through before you begin to make cheese, following the recipes carefully, using the right supplies and ingredients, and reading the tips throughout the book.

As you set off on your cheesemaking journey, rest assured that I have your back should you run into a surprise—but don't focus too much on potential issues because your instincts and the recipes should guide you perfectly. If you do run into trouble, come back and review the tips in this chapter, or email me at claudia@urbancheesecraft.com with Curd Support as the subject line. We'll figure it out together.

> ## "If your creation is delicious, even if it's not what you expected, jot down what happened so you can learn from it and try again."

Zen and the Art of Naming Your Cheese

Yes, you're following a recipe, but as we've discussed, many cheeses were first discovered by accident, so be kind to yourself and tap into your creative side with these *go-with-the-flow* tips. It's quite possible that you'll encounter the challenges laid out in the Troubleshooting section (page 25), but the good news is, you're just as likely to experience none of them! Even in the challenging cases,

REMEMBER: OM = YUM!

though, you can likely eat and enjoy your results. A tough mozzarella (or a tough Chipotle-Lime Oaxaca or Pizza Filata) can be cubed like paneer. (And it will become softer if simmered in a sauce like marinara or curry.) A crumbly ricotta (or Chèvre French Kisses, Fromage Facile, or Classic Cottage Cheese) can still be used like Chivo Fresco, or Farm-Fresh Rounds (pizza, pasta, stuffing veggies, on salads, and so on). My point is, if your creation is delicious, even if it's not what you expected, the thing to do is rename it and jot down what happened so that you learn from it and can try it again.

Keep a Cheese Log

Dedicate a notebook to your cheese journey, like a Ship's Log (and if you don't have one at the ready, turn to page 260 to jot down your first quick notes). As you ride the waves of milk transformation, write about your wild adventures and amazing discoveries. If you liked your "failed" ricotta—quick!—write down what you did to make it happen: Did the milk accidentally boil? Did you add twice as much acid? Maybe you're not sure how this magic happened. Just take careful notes and it may become clear later as you've made more observations.

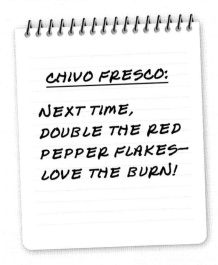

CHIVO FRESCO:

NEXT TIME, DOUBLE THE RED PEPPER FLAKES— LOVE THE BURN!

Aside from this, heed these following words of wisdom (gained through "failures"), and your time making cheese will never be stressful (that would be a shame!).

1. Don't name your cheese until you taste it.

That means, hold off on announcing, "I'm making mozzarella for the first time, y'all! Gather round!" Instead, use the old restaurant trick and sound fancy at the same time by saying, "I'm making Cheese du Jour", or essentially, "Whatever kind I give you!"

AKA "CHEESE OF THE DAY"

When you finish, you can either modify your script . . . ahem, menu . . . to say, "Surprise! I made mozzarella" . . . or, "Here it is, my simple beginner's *Cheese du Jour.*" Okay, that's an elaborate plan. I'm simply saying, don't get too attached, and have fun with the process. Your result will likely be incredibly edible, if not recognizable!

2. Save what looks like a failure to you until you've gathered yourself and some information.

If you ended up not with cheese but with a milky soup instead, save it until you can face it again.

"As you ride the waves of milk transformation, write about your wild adventures and amazing discoveries."

Also, please note that this is incredibly rare. Do not live in fear of the milky soup!

You might be frustrated, and I don't blame you for that. Walk away for a while, but whatever you do, *don't dump out the results.* Put the whole pot in the fridge for a day if you have to. Take a breather. Surprise results can almost always be saved and turned into something delicious.

When your head is clear, retrace your steps: Did you take the plastic cap off your thermometer? (Really, that happens more than you would think!) Double-check your ingredients. Review your notes. Check out the Troubleshooting section. Check my website for FAQs (urbancheesecraft.com). You can even email me at claudia@urbancheesecraft.com with the subject line Curd Support. I like a good challenge, and together we can likely save your cheese or prevent the problem in the future.

3. Finally, get out of your own head.

I have heard from too many aspiring fresh cheesemakers who overthought a recipe. I'm not sure if it's because they assume this process must be far more complicated than it is (or else everyone would do it!), or if it's simply that cheese cravings can mess with your head. Nature wants to please you, so let it! Don't add unnecessary steps because you remember reading something online or recall a factoid from science class. I'm all for encouraging you to play with it later, but when you're learning, follow the carefully crafted recipes contained in these pages.

And if you find an easier method along the way, email me, will ya?

4. Now go make cheese fearlessly.

Free your mind, follow the recipes, and may the curd be with you!

HOW TO USE THIS BOOK AND THE RECIPES

As you make your way through the book, here are a couple of tips to keep in mind and features to look out for as you approach each recipe.

Easy Cheesy Decision

To decide if you have the time, supplies, and use for a particular cheese, refer to the quick summary of facts in the *How Easy Is It?* cheese board on the first page of each recipe. An important factor to consider if you're a novice and want to know where to start is the *Level of Ease*. Because these are all fresh, simple cheeses, they are rated Easy, Easier, and Easiest. Read through each recipe before you make it so you know what's coming, and then follow the photographed step-by-step instructions as you go.

From Gallon to Table

Each of the sixteen cheeses is thoroughly explored via step-by-step instructions, photos, shaping possibilities, serving suggestions, and cheese plate accompaniments. Use the shaping and flavoring ideas (pages 183–211) to learn how one cheese can keep you busy for weeks with variations. Enjoy playing around with DIY pairings and accompaniments (pages 213–233), like baked crackers and drunken fruit.

Prep Like a Chef

Since we are making cheese in one hour, the recipes develop quickly, and your results can be significantly affected if you take ten minutes to find your colander. So, when you've decided which cheese to make, and have the milk and supplies you need, set up a neat workspace and your work flow will be a cinch. Each recipe will give you the information you need (all ingredients and supplies) so that you can customize the basic *mise en place* (professional chef talk for "everything in place") for your own *cheese en place!*

Think Like a Farmer

Am I really asking you to keep that yellowish liquid? Yes, whey! Using all cheesemaking by-products is farm-style resourcefulness at its best. Uses for whey are no exception, and they span the culinary world and beyond. Before allowing a valuable resource to literally go down the drain, consider what you can do with whey. The amount of whey left after making cheese will surprise you, so it's best to be prepared. See the box to the right for some practical uses for bonus whey. (Note: You can freeze it for use later! Just allow about 20 percent space at the top of your container for expansion in the freezer.)

USES FOR ONE-HOUR WHEY

The whey that will result from every cheese recipe will be plentiful. And it still contains minerals and whey protein, so why not use it? It retains a milky flavor with a little tang, making it perfect in several homemade foods.

If you live on a farm, you probably already know that chickens and pigs love whey. I hear that some people feed their plants with it, but since it's quite sweet (and often still a little chunky with curds), I've been afraid to attract ants and critters to my small city lot.

Instead, I focus on keeping it in the kitchen. This is a short list. I'm sure you will find more uses:

- **Smoothies:** What do you think whey protein powder is made of?
- **Risotto, oatmeal, rice, or beans:** Replace water for more nutrition.
- **Soup broth:** It's especially good in cream-style soups.
- **Soaking liquid for beans and grains:** Use instead of plain water, discard after.
- **Ice cream and sorbet:** Substitute whey for 1 cup of the liquid in your recipes.
- **Biscuits, bread, and pizza crust:** Use whey instead of the called for water in any baking recipe.

NOTE: A lot of the lactose is left in the whey so these experiments are not for you if you're barely able to digest the cheese you make! As an alternative, you can always ask if a neighbor can make use of it.

YOU AND A GALLON OF REAL MILK: A SHORT STORY

You have yourself a gallon of whole, raw (cream line) milk. You skim most, but not all, of the cream and use it to make the best butter you'll ever have (page 236). This creates a by-product: real buttermilk. You mix that buttermilk into some batter to make scrumptious pancakes or biscuits.

You still have that low-fat milk you skimmed earlier. Now, you can make a batch of fresh cheese. Pizza Filata (page 151), Chipotle-Lime Oaxaca (page 161), or even Low-Tech Yogurt (page 243) each can be made with low-fat milk.

You will be left with a lot of whey in the process which, in farm quantities, can be used to make old-fashioned ricotta or can be fed to the pigs. But when left with smaller quantities, turn your attention to the "Uses for One-Hour Whey" box, left. Risotto, maybe? Soup? Ice cream?

The moral: One gallon of farm-fresh milk equals a whole host of homemade possibilities. And now you see how that gallon of raw milk is not as expensive as you once thought. . . .

Friend and dairy farmer Mike Guebert

ONE-HOUR CHEESE RECIPES

ARE YOU READY TO AMAZE YOURSELF?

One-hour cheese is accessible to anyone. Even if you consider yourself a novice in the kitchen, do not fear. I have designed the recipes to flow in a natural progression—much like a series of workshops.

So, if you wish to learn cheesemaking as if you were a student in one of my classes, the way to go is to start in the Creamy and Spreadable section and choose a recipe labeled *Easiest*. Then you should move onto a Firm and Chewy cheese of the *Easiest* variety, and end with an *Easiest* Melty and Gooey cheese.

This sequence will give you a great primer in most of the processes we will use, while leaving some additional fun and unique simple steps to discover as you pick and choose your future cheeses with confidence.

Of course, if you have made cheese before, or even if you know your way around the kitchen and have dabbled in all manner of kitchen crafts, go ahead and dig in anywhere. Plus, each recipe has a quick reference guide (look for the "How Easy Is It?" feature) that will assist you in choosing your next cheesy adventure at a glance, so you're covered no matter where you decide to start. Go! Have fun!

MEYER LEMON RICOTTA

Historically speaking, ricotta is made with whey—it's actually a by-product of other cheesemaking. But our batch uses less than a gallon of milk to make ricotta—versus the more typical *500* gallons—so if we used whey, we would only get a few measly teaspoons. Like many smaller operations, we will add milk for a larger yield! This whole milk and cream version will give the traditional whey recipe a run for its money. Further, we will use sweeter Meyer lemons for our acid, imparting a faint, sweet essence that will leave folks guessing.

Its delicate flavor and texture make this ricotta especially wonderful for desserts (cheesecake!) and breakfast favorites (blintzes!) but it also blends nicely in savory dishes with rich sauces. Experiment with half of your batch and add tidbits like herbs, cracked pepper, seeds, dried fruit, and so on, to create a snacking cheese that goes well with crisp veggies or crostini.

HOW EASY IS IT?

LEVEL: Easy   Easier   (Easiest)

READY TO EAT IN:
50 minutes

MAKES: 12 ounces

BIGGEST PAIN: Waiting for the curds to drain slowly.

USES: Include in sweet or savory recipes in need of a mild, semispreadable cheese, like cannoli and lasagna.

RECOMMENDED MILK:
1 quart whole cow's milk and 1 pint cow's milk cream (also called heavy cream or whipping cream)—very flexible; see variations.

WORTH MENTIONING:
This cheese will be very loose when warm and freshly made—chill it in the freezer for 15 minutes to cool it quickly.

INGREDIENTS

2–3 Meyer lemons (¼ cup Meyer lemon juice, plus 2 tablespoons Meyer lemon juice)

1 quart (4 cups) whole cow's milk (*not* ultra-pasteurized)

1 pint (2 cups) cream (*not* ultra-pasteurized)

¼ teaspoon flake salt or to taste

SUPPLIES

Citrus juicer

¼ cup

Small mesh strainer

2-quart stockpot

Large mixing spoon

Cooking thermometer

Large colander or mesh strainer

Fine cheesecloth

Large heat-resistant bowl (for whey collection), optional

¼ teaspoon

1-quart bowl

PRO TIP: Leave the milk at room temperature for 1 to 2 hours so that heating it is faster.

1 Squeeze, strain, and measure ¼ cup lemon juice, plus 2 extra tablespoons. Set the extra tablespoons aside to adjust for varying acidity in Step 7.

4 You may already see some curds forming within seconds. Stay close and monitor the heat, stirring every few minutes to prevent a skin from forming on the milk's surface and to check for sticking milk at the bottom. (Reduce the heat if needed.)

2 Pour the milk and cream into the pot.

3 Pour the lemon juice into the pot and stir thoroughly. Set to medium heat.

5 Check the temperature once you see steam rising from the pot as well as little foam bubbles forming around the edge. Curds will form rapidly as the milk approaches the target temperature of 190°F, and it will look more like thin oatmeal.

6 This is coagulation! Keep checking the temperature, and continue to stir, very gently this time, so that the newly formed curds are not broken up. Turn off the heat when it reaches 190°F.

BE PATIENT, THE LUSCIOUS
TEXTURE DEPENDS ON IT!

7 Take the pot off the burner and allow the curds and whey to sit undisturbed for 10 minutes. If you do not see clear curds and whey, reheat the pot to 190°F, then drizzle in the additional lemon juice, one tablespoon at a time, until coagulation.

8 While you wait, line the colander with cheesecloth. Optional: Place a bowl under the colander to collect the whey (highly recommended—see "Uses for One-Hour Whey," page 31, for ideas). Otherwise, place the lined colander in the sink.

11 Gather the cloth into a bundle and give it a gentle squeeze to strain out that last bit of whey. The whey from this creamy cheese is somewhat milky in appearance. (Compare that to whey for mozzarella, which will be more clear.)

12 Place the cloth full of drained cheese back in the colander, and add the salt.

9 Pour the curds and whey through the cloth.

10 Allow the whey to drain for about 10 minutes or until you get the creamy texture of smooth mashed potatoes.

13 Stir just until the salt is mixed in thoroughly. Salt helps release more whey, and air dries out cheese, so if you stir longer than necessary, the cheese will be crumbly instead of creamy.

14 Stir minimally for the creamiest ricotta! While warm, the consistency will be loose and creamy.

NOTE: Your ricotta may firm up significantly after chilling overnight in the fridge, like all cheeses and fatty foods do. It should become spreadable again with a light stir. If you want a super-rich texture, add a splash of cream just before serving.

15 It's ready to eat! Scoop it into a bowl for eating right away or chill it for a firmer texture.

VARIATIONS + SUBSTITUTIONS

• Use equal amounts of any cow's milk. The creamy texture will decrease with lower fat milk.

• Skip the cream and use all milk.

• Use ¼ cup regular lemon juice, lime juice, or white wine vinegar instead of the Meyer lemon juice.

• Mix any variety of tasty treats into the cheese: fresh or dried oregano, or aromatics like anise seeds, fresh grated nutmeg, or cinnamon. You could even fold in dark chocolate bits after the cheese cools (if it's still warm, you'll end up with milk chocolate–colored ricotta, which would still be yummy, but a little odd looking).

HOLY CANNOLI DIP

— SERVES 4 —

Dip cookies or fruit into it, fill sugar cones with it, or (if you want to be terribly by the book) actually use this dip to stuff cannoli shells. Here's an incredible, and incredibly easy, way to take your Meyer Lemon Ricotta to party time.

1 tablespoon honey or real maple syrup

Zest of 1 organic lemon

Squeeze of lemon juice

1 teaspoon anise seeds

1 to 2 ounces shaved dark chocolate, plus more for garnish if desired

1 cup chilled Meyer Lemon Ricotta

2 tablespoons crushed pistachios (for the topping), optional

Mix the honey, lemon zest, lemon juice, anise, and chocolate into the cup of chilled ricotta. Stir until smooth. Adjust any ingredient to taste. Top with the crushed pistachios and more shaved chocolate, if desired.

Serve it with cookies or biscuits— or ripe fruit (strawberries, apricots, and plums lend a nice contrast). Or, modify the Garlic and Rainbow Pepper Olive Oil Crispbread (page 222) by sprinkling with cinnamon and sugar instead of using garlic, salt, and pepper.

FROMAGE FACILE

Fromage Facile is a mild, creamy, multiuse cheese that is simply great to have on hand. Its name means "easy cheese" in French, and it is: easy to make, easy to use, and easily one of my all-time favorite cheeses. The buttermilk gives it a slight tang, and the result is something between cream cheese and ricotta. Coagulation is swift and visually dramatic for this one, making it an impressive cheese to make with kids or for dinner guests (double the recipe for a crowd): The process is low stress and gratifying. I love dipping garden-grown veggies in a dish of Fromage Facile, but you can also use it for baking—or spreading on breakfast pastries. Alternatively, shape the cheese into a log and cover it with dry herbs; it makes a lovely and delicious hostess gift to bring to a party!

HOW EASY IS IT?

LEVEL: Easy   Easier   (Easiest)

READY TO EAT IN: 30 minutes

MAKES: 6 ounces

BIGGEST PAIN: Squeezing and straining fresh lemon juice.

USES: Great cream cheese, herbed dip, dessert cheese.

RECOMMENDED MILK:
1 quart whole cow's milk and
1 cup cultured buttermilk.

WORTH MENTIONING:
Finding cultured buttermilk (acidic) is important for coagulation.

INGREDIENTS

1 quart (4 cups) whole cow's milk
(*not* ultra-pasteurized)

1 cup cultured buttermilk
(*not* ultra-pasteurized)

2 tablespoons fresh lemon juice

¼ teaspoon flake salt or to taste

Herbs to taste, optional

SUPPLIES

Medium colander or mesh strainer

Fine cheesecloth

Large heat-resistant bowl
(for whey collection), optional

2-quart stockpot

Cooking thermometer

Large mixing spoon

1 cup

1 tablespoon

¼ teaspoon

Parchment paper

1 Line the colander with cheesecloth, wet or dry. Place a bowl underneath if you want to collect the whey (see page 31 for "Uses for One-Hour Whey"); otherwise, place the lined colander in your clean sink.

4 When the milk temperature hits 175°F, add the buttermilk and lemon juice and stir thoroughly. You should start seeing some coagulation!

CURD ALERT!

2 Pour the quart of cow's milk into the pot. Then heat the milk at medium to 175°F.

3 Stay close and monitor the heat, stirring every few minutes to prevent a skin from forming on the surface of the milk. Check, too, for sticking milk at the bottom of the pot. (Reduce the heat if you feel any milk sticking.)

5 Once you've completely stirred in the buttermilk and lemon juice, take the pot off the heat. Leave it undisturbed for 5 minutes.

6 Return to the cooling pot. You will clearly see a separation between curds and whey now. Stir the curds gently for a few seconds just to check out the change in texture. Then pour the curds and whey into the cloth-lined colander.

7 Allow the curds to drain until they resemble thick oatmeal; it should take just 1 to 2 minutes. Stir in the salt.

8 Pack the cheese into a paper-lined dish to form it into a wheel.

yum.

9 Flip the dish onto the serving platter and peel away the paper. Your Fromage Facile is ready to eat!

VARIATIONS + SUBSTITUTIONS

- Mix in fresh herbs, sun-dried tomatoes (no oil), or pickled jalapeños to make a nice bagel spread.

- Add currants, diced dried apricots, or any other dried fruit you enjoy.

- Cool the cheese in a jar and gift it!

NO-BAKE CHEESE TARTLET

— MAKES TWO 4-INCH TARTLETS —

I'm a sucker for French pastries, especially tarts covered in piles of juicy fruit. This is my simple, fresh version that you can whip up in 5 minutes. Adjust the sweetness in the crust and filling to taste and change out the fruit depending on what's at the farmers' market.

2 tablespoons honey or real maple syrup

1 cup Fromage Facile

¼ teaspoon ground cinnamon
or nutmeg, optional

½ cup roasted and salted almonds

¼ cup juicy medjool dates, pitted

1 cup total berries, chopped melon,
peaches, and/or plums

1 tablespoon orange marmalade or honey
(for shiny fruit), optional

FILLING: Mix honey or real maple syrup with Fromage Facile (then you can fancy it up with anything you enjoy: cinnamon, nutmeg . . .).

CRUST: Use a food processor to coarsely crush the almonds and ¼ cup pitted medjool dates. The crust mix should appear crumbly but stay formed when squeezed. If necessary, add another date to help form the crust. Press crust evenly into two 4-inch pans. Spread cheese filling over the crusts.

TOPPING: Decorate the tarts with fruit and dot them with the marmalade or honey.

Your tart is ready to eat right away—or chill it for half an hour so that it slices neatly.

CHÈVRE FRENCH KISSES

This recipe is my homage to a French-style chèvre covered in Herbes de Provence (aromatic herbs including lavender), but I decided to *infuse* the milk with fresh herbs as it warmed so that you end up with the floral flavors of summer in France (I imagine, I haven't been!), without the fibrous bite of dried herbs and flowers (not so cute between the teeth). To stay truly Provençal or in the French country style, we shape the little kisses by hand for tempting bites, perfect for a cheese platter for two.

Of course, this is how I like to make these kisses, but you can pick up where I left off and use other herbs, spices, and even dried fruit to get different, but no less enticing, results. And though I enjoy the small bites, you can opt to leave this chèvre as a spread or shape it into logs (see page 188).

HOW EASY IS IT?

LEVEL: Easy (Easier) Easiest

READY TO EAT IN: 45 minutes

MAKES: Little less than ½ pound

BIGGEST PAIN: Old or low-quality pasteurized goat's milk can be difficult to coagulate.

USES: Filling for tarts and quiche, crumbled over roasted veggies or salad, or just as a spreadable cheese.

RECOMMENDED MILK: ½ gallon goat's milk and 1 cup cow's milk cream (also called heavy cream or whipping cream).

WORTH MENTIONING: The curd is easier to shape by hand when cooled slightly.

INGREDIENTS

½ gallon goat's milk
(*not* ultra-pasteurized)

1 cup cream
(*not* ultra-pasteurized)

4 to 6 fresh sprigs organic
herbs like lavender, basil,
sage, thyme, and rosemary,
washed thoroughly and
patted dry

¼ cup white wine vinegar

1 teaspoon flake salt or to taste

PRO TIP:
Leave the milk
at room temperature
for 1 to 2 hours so
that heating it is
faster.

SUPPLIES

1 cup

3-quart stockpot

Cooking thermometer

Large mixing spoon

Slotted spoon or mesh spider (optional)

¼ cup

Large colander or mesh strainer

Fine cheesecloth

Large heat-resistant bowl
(optional, for whey collection)

1 teaspoon

1 Pour the milk and cream into the pot.

4 Dip the thermometer in and start checking the temperature when you see steam and little foam bubbles forming. (Note: Do not let the milk boil, or your creamy cheese will become firm.)

AREN'T THEY PRETTY?

2 Add the washed herbs right into the milk. Then turn the heat to medium.

3 Stay close and monitor the heat, stirring every few minutes to prevent a skin from forming on the surface of the milk, and to check for sticking milk at the bottom of the pot. (Reduce heat if you feel any milk sticking.)

5 Just before the milk reaches 185°F, scoop out the herbs.

6 When the milk reaches 185°F, add the vinegar and stir it in thoroughly with just seven quick strokes.

7 Lower the heat to the lowest setting. Gently stir the milk every few seconds for 2 minutes; you do not want to break up any newly forming curds, so do not stir vigorously or continuously.

8 You should see coagulation after 1 minute. If you do not, heat for up to 2 minutes longer.

11 After 10 minutes, you should see an increase in curd formation.

12 Pour the curds and whey through the cheesecloth and allow the whey to drain for about 10 minutes or until the curds are the creamy texture of smooth mashed potatoes.

9 Take the pot off the burner and allow the curds and whey to sit undisturbed for 10 minutes.

10 Line the colander with the cheesecloth, and place the colander over a bowl if you will reserve the whey (see "Uses for One-Hour Whey," page 31), or in your clean sink if you will not.

13 Add salt and stir thoroughly. This flavors the cheese but also helps drain the last of the whey.

14 The whey that is left behind will appear more milky than in other recipes. This is normal for this creamy goat cheese. See "Uses for One-Hour Whey" (page 31) for suggestions on how to use this rich by-product.

15 After cooling a little, your goat cheese is ready to shape. Scoop out little two-bite portions of cheese with your fingers and smooth them into balls in your hands.

16 Pinch the top of each cheese ball and flatten the bottom when you place it on a platter; your Chèvre French Kisses are ready to serve and eat as is, or they can be decorated with leftover herbs or edible flowers (see page 206).

VARIATIONS + SUBSTITUTIONS

- Use any fresh or dried herbs you have on hand to infuse the milk: Mint, chives, dill, or parsley each create delicious results—or experiment with combinations to make new flavor discoveries!

- Mix minced herbs into the curd or cover the kisses in herbs or spices once they're shaped. Lavender flowers and tiny thyme leaves are especially pretty and delicious.

- Make every kiss different: Add honey to one, cranberries to another, and mint to another. Keep a variety of tastes and colors in mind.

- Omit the cream for a lighter cheese with a slightly more goaty flavor. (Note: The yield will decrease, so adjust as necessary.)

SIZZLING PEACHES AND GREENS

— SERVES 4 —

Ripe juicy white peaches, arugula, butter, balsamic vinegar—yum. Every one of these ingredients is delicious on its own. Put them together and you have a recipe for seduction: Here's to impressing the pants off people! That came out weird.

2 ripe white peaches (yellow will also work)

2 teaspoons good balsamic vinegar

1 teaspoon butter (page 236)

2 cups arugula or mixed salad greens

4 Chèvre French Kiss cheeses

2 teaspoons pine nuts (for the topping), optional

Cut the peaches in half and remove the stones. Brush or drizzle each cut peach half with balsamic vinegar. Preheat a cast-iron skillet or grill pan. Butter the pan and place the peaches, cut-side down, on the hot skillet (listen to them sizzle!). Sear the peaches just until the balsamic vinegar caramelizes and the butter is fragrant. Look for some browning if you lift a peach. Be careful to not let it burn, though—it's a fine line. Place ½ cup of the arugula greens on a plate and a peach half, seared-side up, on top. Top with a Chèvre French Kiss cheese in the middle. Drizzle more of the balsamic vinegar over the cheese. Garnish the dish with pine nuts, if available.

CLASSIC COTTAGE CHEESE

Whenever I mention cottage cheese in one of my classes, Little Miss Muffet inevitably comes up, since her curds and whey were likely to have resembled cottage cheese. Cottage cheese is a nostalgic treat for many whose references range from Mother Goose to Jazzercise, but don't dismiss this cheese as simply old-fashioned or you'll miss out on its versatility and satisfying tang. This batch is generous in size so you can enjoy a scoop with ripe fresh fruit, mix it into pancake batter, and use it in lasagna all in one week.

So, trust me, you don't have to be a Jazzercise fan to enjoy cottage cheese, though it won't hurt to get out those leg-warmers and turn up your favorite 1980s tunes. You know you want to.

HOW EASY IS IT?

LEVEL: (Easy) Easier Easiest

READY TO EAT IN: 1 hour

MAKES: 1½ pounds

BIGGEST PAIN: Extra ice-bath process at the end.

USES: Lasagna, pancakes, salad topping, fruit accompaniment, dips.

RECOMMENDED MILK:
1 gallon whole cow's milk and 1¼ cups cultured buttermilk (flexible; see variations).

WORTH MENTIONING:
The cultured buttermilk offers the classic cottage cheese flavor in a short amount of time. It can easily be replaced with other milks, but the cheese will lose the characteristic tangy flavor.

INGREDIENTS

1¼ cups cultured buttermilk
(*not* ultra-pasteurized)

¼ tablet vegetarian rennet

½ cup cool dechlorinated water

1 gallon whole cow's milk
(*not* ultra-pasteurized)

3 cups ice cubes

1 teaspoon flake salt or to taste

SUPPLIES

¼ cup

½ cup

5-quart stockpot

Large whisk

Cooking thermometer

Fine cheesecloth

Large colander or mesh strainer

Large heat-resistant bowl
(for whey collection), optional

Large mixing spoon

Knife, optional

Large bowl for ice bath

1 teaspoon

1 cup

1 Measure ¼ cup of the buttermilk. Reserve the rest.

4 Whisk the buttermilk into the milk and heat both on medium to 95°F.

2 Dissolve the ¼ tablet of rennet in the ½ cup of cool water and set aside.

3 Pour the milk into the pot.

5 Add the rennet solution to the milk and mix it in with 20 quick strokes to make sure the rennet is incorporated evenly.

6 Turn off the heat, set the pot away from the stove, and cover it. Do not disturb for 15 minutes.

7 Use this time to prepare a cloth-lined colander and bowl if you want to collect the whey (see page 21); otherwise, place the lined colander in your clean sink.

CLOSE-UP

Ideally, the curd will pull away from the edge of the pot as one "solid" mass.

8 After 15 minutes, you should have a pot of curd that looks like yogurt. The curd should pull away from the edges when you press it with the back of your spoon, but yogurtlike curd pieces floating in clearish whey work, too.

11 The curds will shrink as they cook and as you move them in the hot whey. You want to end up with almond-size curds.

12 Scoop curds from the bottom of the pot and cut any larger pieces, as shown, so they cook evenly.

9 Use the spoon or a knife to chop large pieces of curd into 1-inch chunks, but do not stir yet.

10 Turn the heat back on to medium and allow the curds to cook for 1 minute, then gently move the chunks around while heating to 115°F (do not break up the curds by stirring too vigorously, however).

13 When you see the proper size, lower the heat to maintain it at 115°F as you move the chunks of curd in the hot whey and check that they have changed from yogurt texture to scrambled egg texture (this can take 5 to 15 minutes).

14 Scoop up a couple of curd pieces in a spoon and pinch them to check their consistency: They should feel a little springy, and not dissolve easily. If they dissolve, continue heating and moving the curds around, then "pinch check" every minute.

15 Turn off the heat when all of the curd appears to be an even consistency. This step will become faster as you get more experienced in observing changes and regulating heat.

16 Pour the curds and whey into the colander.

19 Prepare an ice bath by mixing the ice cubes and cold tap water in a large bowl.

20 Gather the curd-filled cheesecloth and dunk it into the cold water while holding the ends like a loose bag. The cold shock will form the curds so that they don't fuse back together like ricotta.

17 Allow the curds to drain and cool for 3 to 5 minutes before digging in with clean hands.

THIS IS CALLED "MILLING" THE CURDS.

18 Mix the curds gently and break them down to the size curd you would like in your cheese: They can be as large as almonds or as small as sunflower seeds, but note that they will continue to shrink in the next steps.

21 Move the bag back and forth in the ice bath to ensure that all the curds get the cold treatment. When the curds feel thoroughly cool, twist and squeeze the cloth to wring out excess water.

22 Unwrap the curds and empty them into a clean bowl.

23 Use a spoon or your hands to gently break up the curds that became compressed when you squeezed the cloth. Add salt and the reserved 1 cup of buttermilk, and stir thoroughly.

24 Your homemade cottage cheese is ready to serve.

YOU DID IT, YOU MADE A CLASSIC!

- To add moisture and different creamy and tangy flavors, substitute about ½ cup of cream, milk, or yogurt (to taste) for the buttermilk in Step 23.

- Use low-fat or skim milk instead of whole milk.

- Add 2 tablespoons lemon juice to the milk instead of the initial ¼ cup buttermilk.

- Mix in lemon zest and diced fresh fruit (like pineapple or peaches) for an ambrosia-like salad or, for a decidedly savory treat, mix in minced fresh herbs (like parsley and chives) with an extra pinch of salt.

GROWN-UP AND GRILLED PINEAPPLE

— SERVES 2 —

This one's for my mom, who, when I was a kid, used to indulge in some seriously complex cottage cheese fruit salads from Mexican fruit stands. The stands are like shrines to fruit: juices, smoothies, fruit pops, and fruit salads in tropical combinations. She's lucky my palate found her salads too sweet and fussy then, so she had those all to herself! My modern interpretation keeps it simple but has just enough depth to make it special.

2 pineapple rings
1 cup Classic Cottage Cheese
2 teaspoons sunflower seeds
2 teaspoons currants (or raisins)
2 teaspoons honey

Butcher a pineapple (it's easier than it looks) by hacking off parts you can't eat. Slice the pineapple into rings ½ inch thick. I like the pineapple core, but if it's too fibrous for you (as it is for many), cut it out ring by ring to try to keep the rings intact. Set aside 2 rings and refrigerate the rest for eating later. Place the pineapple slices on a hot grill until you see some nice grill marks. You can also broil or even pan-sear the pineapple. Top each grilled pineapple ring with a ½-cup scoop of your homemade cottage cheese. Sprinkle evenly with sunflower seeds, currants, and a drizzle of honey. Boom.

CURRIED PANEER

Paneer is a farmer's cheese used extensively in Indian cuisine as an affordable and vegetarian protein. You may have seen it floating in curries and wondered if it's tofu. It is not, but it behaves in much the same way. It does not melt and it takes on the flavor of whatever it is paired with, making it a natural for stews and stir-fries. Paneer and curry go so well together, why not merge them for a curried paneer?! In this recipe, the milk is simmered with curry powder so as to infuse it with the flavor from the start. You can of course omit it and make plain paneer to use in saag paneer (spinach and cheese) and other traditional Indian dishes, but as you will see in the serving suggestion, this version is something special when panfried.

I used lime juice in a bottle because it is so often preferred to fresh for its nonperishability, but you can use fresh lime juice or any of the acids we discussed in the pantry section in equal proportion. Paneer can also be made with goat's milk, or half cow's milk and half goat's milk. It's a "use what you have" kind of cheese. Always handy when you ask, "What's for dinner?!"

HOW EASY IS IT?

LEVEL: Easy   Easier   (Easiest)

READY TO EAT IN: 1 hour

MAKES: More than 1 pound

BIGGEST PAIN: High temperatures require attention to avoid your pot scorching and boiling over.

USES: In stews, stir-fry, salads, or curries; use it as a protein as you would tofu or chicken.

RECOMMENDED MILK: 1 gallon whole cow's milk (very flexible; see variations).

WORTH MENTIONING: It is very easy to cut this recipe to make just a half or quarter batch.

INGREDIENTS

½ cup lime juice (plus 2 extra tablespoons
   to adjust for varying acidity)

1 gallon whole cow's milk
   (*not* ultra-pasteurized)

2 tablespoons curry powder

1 teaspoon flake salt
   or to taste

SUPPLIES

½ cup

1 tablespoon

Large colander or mesh strainer

Fine cheesecloth

Large heat-resistant bowl
   (for whey collection), optional

5-quart stockpot

Large whisk

Cooking thermometer

Large mixing spoon

Small flat plate

Milk gallon jug with water,
   for pressing cheese

PRO TIP:
Leave the milk
at room temperature
for 1 to 2 hours so
that heating it is
faster.

1 Measure ½ cup lime juice and keep the extra 2
tablespoons handy.

4 Add the curry powder
to the milk and whisk or
stir thoroughly.

SWIRLY!

2 Line your colander with cheesecloth. Place a bowl underneath if you want to collect the whey (see "Uses for One-Hour Whey," page 31); otherwise, place the lined colander in your clean sink.

3 Pour the milk into the pot. Set aside the empty gallon to use later as a press weight.

5 Heat the milk, on medium, to 200°F—almost to a boil. Stay close and monitor the heat, stirring every few minutes to prevent a skin from forming on the surface of the milk and to check for sticking milk at the bottom. (Reduce the heat if you feel any milk sticking.)

6 Look for steam and frothy bubbles as the milk approaches 200°F. (Note: Watch carefully because this is close to boiling temperature.) Add the lime juice when you reach 200°F, and stir well.

DON'T BREAK THEM UP, JUST MOVE THEM AROUND.

7 Coagulation should happen within seconds—and it is dramatic, so if you do not see it right away, confirm the temperature and add more lime juice, a tablespoon at a time, until you see coagulation.

8 When coagulation has occurred, lower the heat and gently stir the curds for 2 minutes. Stirring assists the curds in shrinking and releasing whey, which will make the paneer firm.

10 Add the salt and stir thoroughly but quickly. The salt and exposure to air promote the release of whey and dry out the curds; being quick will still result in a soft enough curd that can be tightly compressed.

11 As you stir, adjust the salt to taste. If you plan to soak the curried paneer in a pungent sauce, add less. If you plan to snack on it plain, you may want more.

9 Gently spoon or pour the curds into the cheesecloth and let them drain for 3 to 5 minutes or until they resemble firm scrambled eggs. Stir them gently to help release whey.

LIME TIME!

Fresh lime juice acidity will vary and different brands of bottled lime juice will also vary (some contain more water—and even sugar!) so try to find a pure lime juice so that your measurements are accurate. You can make cheese with the lime juice you have regardless, you may just have to pour a little more in if you don't see coagulation at the right time. Is your curd too tangy? Rinse it in cool tap water as it drains and you will wash off some of that acid.

12 Gather the cheesecloth corners and twist them to create a tight bundle, then squeeze to release more whey.

13 Press the curd bag into the colander (now the mold) and firmly place a small, flat plate or lid on top.

14 Fill the empty milk gallon with water and use it as a weight on top of the plate. Press the paneer for at least 15 minutes. The longer it presses and cools, the firmer the paneer will be.

15 Unwrap the Curried Paneer, and it's ready to eat or use in recipes—immediately! (Cooling the paneer in the fridge overnight after pressing will firm it up substantially but in a pinch, a flash cooling in the freezer for 10 minutes will help.)

NOTE: Browning cubes of paneer in ghee or coconut oil helps them remain nice and firm in stir-fries, fajitas, sauces, and curries.

VARIATIONS + SUBSTITUTIONS

- Use low-fat or skim milk: The paneer will not be as creamy for snacking but will soften plenty when cooked and will remain firm in sauces.

- Use lemon juice or white wine vinegar in place of the lime juice.

- As mentioned above, you can skip the curry powder and make this plain: It results in a very versatile protein for sweet and savory dishes alike.

- Replace the curry powder with any herbs or spices you like—cracked black pepper, turmeric, or even rosemary!

CURRY IN A HURRY LETTUCE WRAPS

— MAKES 2 TO 4 WRAPS; SERVES 2 —

Do you ever crave the flavor of curry in summer but don't feel like simmering a stew in hot weather? These wraps fit the bill! Take them to work (pack the makings and assemble them right before eating) for a nice upgrade from a turkey sandwich.

1 cup cubed Curried Paneer

4 tablespoons ghee (page 240), or coconut oil for frying

Sea salt to taste

Dash of cayenne pepper, optional

2 large (or 4 small) butter or romaine lettuce leaves

4 tablespoons plain yogurt

Brown cubes of Curried Paneer in the ghee or coconut oil (let them get crispy before you flip them so they don't stick). Blot them if necessary, and sprinkle with sea salt (and a dash of cayenne if you like heat). Tuck the golden cubes into the large leaves of washed and dried lettuce (you can try chard or kale if you like hardier greens). Top them off with dollops of tangy yogurt (which you can make yourself, page 243!) and wrap them into little bundles.

Options: Try with tomato, mango, or cilantro chutney or go full hippie and use a peeler to make strips of cucumber, carrot, jicama, daikon, apples, beets, or any other firm veggie or fruit you enjoy. Toss the strips in lime juice and a bit of salt and tuck everything into the wrap. Healthy *and* indulgent!

CHIVO FRESCO

Y ou may have noticed that many cheeses in the dairy aisle fall under the name *chèvre*. The word simply means "goat" in French, and refers to a wide variety of cheeses made from goat's milk. In Spanish, the word for "goat" is *chivo*. Queso fresco ("fresh cheese") is a mild cheese made from cow's milk that is often crumbled onto tostadas or enchiladas at Mexican restaurants. So, our Chivo Fresco translates to "fresh goat"—always a good thing, in my opinion. You could say this is the cheese that results when chèvre and queso fresco have a spicy baby.

If you think you don't like goat cheese, you might be surprised by this mild version: In the European tradition of combining milks, I used half cow's milk and half goat's milk for a more delicate flavor, but the combo also enhances coagulation and yield. That said, you can easily make a more conventional queso fresco with 100 percent cow's milk. In the tradition of quesos enchilados (chili-rubbed cheeses), I added red pepper flakes to this recipe, but you can leave it plain or add whatever you suspect will make it exciting: chives, garlic powder, Creole spice blend?

HOW EASY IS IT?

LEVEL: Easy   Easier   (Easiest)

READY TO EAT IN: 40 minutes

MAKES: About 10 ounces

BIGGEST PAIN: High temperatures require attention to avoid scorching and boiling over.

USES: Crumble or slice onto most anything, especially Latin dishes. Use it warm and just-drained to stuff roasted veggies or pasta shells.

RECOMMENDED MILK: 1 quart whole cow's milk and 1 quart goat's milk (very flexible; see variations).

WORTH MENTIONING: Press it like Curried Paneer (page 67) for a firm cheese or use/store it immediately after draining for a semicreamy cheese.

INGREDIENTS

1 quart (4 cups) whole cow's milk
(*not* ultra-pasteurized)

1 quart (4 cups) goat's milk
(*not* ultra-pasteurized)

¼ cup apple cider vinegar

1 teaspoon flake salt or to taste

1 teaspoon chili pepper flakes
or to taste

SUPPLIES

Large colander or mesh strainer

Fine cheesecloth

Large heat-resistant bowl
(for whey collection), optional

3-quart stockpot

Cooking thermometer

Large mixing spoon

¼ cup

1 teaspoon

Cheese mold of choice
(to shape a wheel), optional

Clean 16-ounce jar or bottle,
for pressing cheese

1 Line the colander with cheesecloth. Place a bowl underneath if you want to collect the whey (see "Uses for One-Hour Whey," page 31); otherwise, place the lined colander in your clean sink.

4 When the temperature reaches 200°F, add the apple cider vinegar and stir it in thoroughly.

2 Pour both quarts of milk into the pot and heat the milk, on medium, to 200°F.

3 Stay close and monitor the heat, stirring every few minutes to prevent a skin from forming on the surface of the milk. Check for sticking milk at the bottom of the pot. (Reduce the heat if you feel any milk sticking.)

5 Coagulation should happen within seconds.

CURD ALERT!

6 Take the pot off the hot burner and very gently stir the curds for 1 minute (don't break them up, just move them around as they shrink and release more whey).

7 Pour the curds and whey into the cloth-lined colander. Let the curds drain for 2 to 5 minutes, stirring gently to release whey, until the curds resemble thick oatmeal.

8 Add the salt and the chili pepper flakes to the curds (you may do this in the colander, or transfer the curds to a bowl).

11 Squeeze the bundle into any one of the molds mentioned in the Equipment section (page 10), as shown. Here, I use a plastic ricotta basket to create a wheel shape.

12 Press the curd bag into the mold, and fold the cloth neatly on top.

9 Stir thoroughly to further cool and dry the curds. The salt and exposure to air both promote whey release, so being quick will still result in a soft enough curd that can be tightly compressed. But, if you want dry crumbles, stir as much as you'd like!

10 Gather the corners of the cheesecloth to create a tight bundle. You can press the cheese right in the colander (as demonstrated in the Curried Paneer recipe, page 67) or . . .

13 Firmly place a clean, water-filled 16-ounce jar or bottle on top, for about 15 minutes. More whey will drain from the mold.

14 Remove the press and unwrap your beautiful wheel.

15 Your Chivo Fresco is ready to crumble onto tacos or to eat with cucumbers or tortilla chips and guacamole right away. The longer it cools, however, the easier it will be to slice.

• Skip the chili pepper flakes, or replace them with fresh or dried herbs, cracked pepper, or finely chopped roasted garlic.

• Add smoked salt instead of regular salt for a hearty flavor boost.

• Use 100 percent cow's milk or 100 percent goat's milk (use a double layer of cheesecloth when using all goat's milk since its curds tend to be very small).

• After it cools and firms, slice and fry the Chivo Fresco like Curried Paneer (see page 67).

• Stop after Step 9 before you press the cheese, and use the cheese in crumble form.

MEXICAN BÁNH MÌ (TORTA!)

— MAKES 2 SANDWICHES; SERVES 2 —

The first time I tried a bánh mì (Vietnamese sub sandwich), I instantly fell for the familiar yet exotic combinations. I grew up eating tortas (Mexican subs), with cilantro and spicy peppers; bánh mì are similar but definitely have their own awesome characteristics. In this serving suggestion, I'm offering up the best of both—and the result is delicious. As my partner, Jeff, would say, my arm is sore from all of the pats on the back I'm giving myself.

2 petite baguettes
2 teaspoons mayonnaise
½ cup crumbled Chivo Fresco
½ avocado, sliced
8 pickled or fresh jalapeño pieces
½ cucumber, cut into thin strips
8 sprigs cilantro

Slice the crusty baguettes*, spread them with mayo, and then fill them with the Chivo Fresco, avocado slices, pickled jalapeños (canned rajas en escabeche if you can find them; if not, fresh are good, if you can handle the heat), strips of cucumbers, and cilantro.

   To add heft, scour the fridge for leftover barbecued chicken, tempeh "bacon," or tuna salad and stuff them in, too.

Don't eat wheat? Fry a corn tortilla in coconut oil and top with the same goodies for a piled-high tostada. (Cross-cultural name not required.)

HONEYED TOAST CHEESE

My inspiration for this recipe is the Finnish cheese juustoleipä (also known as bread cheese), a precooked cheese originally made of reindeer milk that can be dunked in coffee and eaten for breakfast like toast. I couldn't pass up the opportunity to play with *that* idea!

I infused this incarnation with cardamom flavor (which is not Finnish, but is inspired by ras malai, an Indian treat made with paneer and flavored with cardamom syrup), which adds a warm spiciness on a chilly day.

When it's allowed to cool or is just toasted slightly, this cow's milk version is like buttered toast. Freshly broiled, Honeyed Toast Cheese tastes like and has the consistency of a ricotta cheesecake. Top it with juicy berries to enjoy as a delicious dessert, or do like the Finnish and have it take a dive into your coffee!

HOW EASY IS IT?

LEVEL: (Easy) Easier Easiest

READY TO EAT IN: 1 hour

MAKES: ½ pound

BIGGEST PAIN: Extra broiling step, which means more dirty dishes.

USES: As toast, as cheesecake, or in place of a crust for a fruit tart.

RECOMMENDED MILK: ½ gallon whole cow's milk (very flexible; see variations).

WORTH MENTIONING: You can broil it right before serving as instructed or skip broiling. The cheese will firm up just by cooling and will be similar to paneer (see page 67), but sweet.

INGREDIENTS

1 cinnamon stick

10 cardamom pods

½ gallon cow's milk (*not* ultra-pasteurized)

¼ cup apple cider vinegar

¼ teaspoon flake salt or to taste

2 tablespoons honey, divided

3 tablespoons butter

SUPPLIES

Mortar and pestle

3-inch length of cotton twine

4 x 4-inch piece of cheesecloth
    or coffee filter

Large colander or mesh strainer

Fine cheesecloth

Large heat-resistant bowl
    (for whey collection), optional

3-quart stockpot

Large mixing spoon

Cooking thermometer

¼ cup

¼ teaspoon

Medium mixing bowl, for curds

1 tablespoon

8-inch cast-iron skillet or
    oven-safe dish

1 spoon, for pressing cheese

Small heat-resistant bowl

NOTE: This cheese is ready to eat at the end of Part 1, or you can refrigerate it until you are ready for Part 2. With practice, Parts 1 and 2 add up to an hour or less.

OR MASH WITH THE BASE OF A MUG!

1 Crush the cinnamon and cardamom pods with a mortar and pestle to release their oils and aroma.

4 Pour the milk into the pot.

LIKE A
HOMEMADE
TEA BAG

2 Collect and tie the spices into the small piece of cheesecloth or coffee filter to create a bundle. Set it aside.

3 Line the colander with cheesecloth. Place a bowl underneath if you want to collect the whey (see "Uses for One-Hour Whey," page 31); otherwise, place the lined colander in your clean sink.

5 Drop the bundle of spices into the pot of milk. Then heat the milk, on medium, to 200°F.

6 Stay close and monitor the heat, stirring every few minutes to prevent a skin from forming on the surface of the milk. Check for sticking milk at the bottom of the pot. (Reduce the heat if you feel any milk sticking.)

7 Look for steam and frothy bubbles as the milk approaches 200°F. (Note: It should look like foam, not a rolling boil.) Remove the bundle of spices just as the milk reaches temperature.

8 Confirm that the milk temperature has reached 200°F.

11 Turn off the heat and carefully pour the curds and whey into the cloth-lined colander.

12 Drain the curds for 3 to 5 minutes or until their texture resembles popcorn. You may stir them gently to help release whey.

DON'T SEE THIS? DRIZZLE MORE VINEGAR TILL YOU DO!

9 Add and stir in the apple cider vinegar. Within seconds, coagulation should happen—and it is dramatic. (If for some reason it is not obvious, add another tablespoon of apple cider vinegar; some brands can be a little weaker.)

10 Lower the heat and gently stir the curds for 2 minutes (don't break them up, just move them around). Stirring assists them in shrinking and releasing whey, which will make the Toast Cheese firm.

13 Add the salt and stir it in quickly and thoroughly.

14 Gather the cheesecloth corners and twist them to create a tight bundle, squeezing to release more whey.

15 Unwrap the curds and place them in the medium-size mixing bowl. Mix in one tablespoon of the honey. (Note: Honey varies in color from a pale creamy hue to a deep molasses color. Experiment—they'll all provide slightly nuanced flavors.)

16 Use your hands to knead the curds into a doughlike texture, about a minute. You will know it's the right consistency when a handful clumps together. Your cheese is ready to eat warm now (try it on toast with jam on top) or store for later.

3 Use a spoon to press the doughy cheese into the skillet immediately.

4 Pour the remaining honey butter over the flattened cheese. Most will soak into the cheese as it heats in the next step, with some remaining at the top.

1 Melt the butter and remaining honey in a skillet, about 1 minute.

2 Pour the melted honey butter into a small bowl. Leave the residual coating in the skillet.

5 Broil, brown with a culinary torch, or bake in a preheated oven at 450°F until the top gets toasty and the butter and honey is absorbed, about 15 minutes. Allow cheese to cool in the pan.

6 Invert the skillet over a cutting board or other work surface, allowing the cheese to fall, top-side down. The bottom should appear toasted as well. (Note: If you torched it, leave it in the skillet to slice—the bottom will not have browned.)

7 Slice up the cooled cheese and, using a fork, dunk a slice into your coffee. Make sure you *Finnish* the whole cup!

• Replace the cardamom with powdered cinnamon and the honey with maple syrup to make French Toast Cheese!

• Continue to play with the spices: Try ground or whole cloves, star anise, or nutmeg.

• Knead in small bits of dried fruit before broiling: apricots, currants, apples, and so on.

• Use low-fat or skim milk. Low-fat Toast Cheese is very firm, but it makes a good grain-free crust for fruit tarts when chilled.

• Swap out the skillet for small ramekins to make single-portion "cakes" to top with crushed fresh berries.

• Knead the curd into patties for small stackable cakes and pan fry them in butter. Drizzle them with honey while still warm!

STRAWBERRY-COVERED CHOCOLATE CHEESECAKE

— SERVES 4 —

Everyone knows and loves chocolate-covered strawberries, but what about strawberry-covered chocolate? On top of a cheesecake! That totally wins.

- 2 ounces dark chocolate
- 1 pan (or 3 small patties) Honeyed Toast Cheese
- 5 to 8 ripe strawberries, washed and sliced

Shave the dark chocolate using a cheese grater (of course!) onto the hot Toast Cheese at Step 6 in Part 2. If you are using cooled cheese, melt the chocolate and spread or drizzle it over the cheese. Press sliced strawberries into the melted chocolate. Eat immediately or better yet, chill the cheesecake in the freezer for 15 minutes or until the chocolate firms up and holds the strawberries. Serve with strong hot or iced coffee.

HALOUMI? HALOU-YOU!

aloumi has been appearing more and more frequently in grocery stores under the new-fangled title "Grilling Cheese." It's a little sad that we traded in the traditional name for a marketable one, but it also means that many more people are now willing to take a chance on haloumi, which is a good thing. And the marketing teams are correct: Haloumi, the Great Grilling (i.e., nonmelting) Cheese is ideal on the grill, broiled, or panfried in a nice hot skillet. Its salty, firm, chewy qualities pair perfectly with refreshing summer veggies. Skip the oregano and make it plain, or mix in the more traditional mint or any other herbs and spices that tickle your fancy.

There is considerable debate about the origin of this cheese, and equally interesting arguments claim its roots are in Cyprus, Greece, or Lebanon. The takeaway, though, is that if there's such a fight to claim this cheese, you should probably try it right away and see what all the fuss is about.

HOW EASY IS IT?

LEVEL: Easy (Easier) Easiest

READY TO EAT IN: 1 hour

MAKES: ½ pound

BIGGEST PAIN: Finding a large enough microwave-safe bowl for the curds and whey that also fits in the microwave.

USES: Grilling, broiling, panfrying.

RECOMMENDED MILK: 1 quart whole milk, 1 quart goat's milk.

WORTH MENTIONING: The recipe relies on microwave use; alternate instructions for heating and stretching are provided, but may take longer.

INGREDIENTS

¼ tablet vegetarian rennet

¼ cup dechlorinated water

1 quart (4 cups) whole cow's milk
(*not* ultra-pasteurized)

1 quart (4 cups) goat's milk
(*not* ultra-pasteurized)

2 teaspoons flake salt

1 teaspoon dried oregano

SUPPLIES

¼ cup

3-quart stockpot

Cooking thermometer

Large whisk

Large spoon

Knife, optional

Large colander or mesh strainer

Fine cheesecloth

Large heat-resistant bowl
(for whey collection), optional

Large microwave-safe bowl
(3-quart capacity)

1 teaspoon

Small loaf pan or other cheese mold

1 Dissolve the ¼ tablet of rennet in the ¼ cup water and set it aside.

CURD ALERT!

4 Continue heating the milk to 110°F until you see a separation between curds and whey when a spoon is inserted. The curd will look similar to yogurt, and the whey will be a milky light yellow.

2 Pour both quarts of milk into the pot and heat on medium to 95°F.

3 As soon as the temperature reaches 95°F, add the rennet solution. Use a whisk or spoon to mix it in with 15 quick strokes to make sure it is incorporated evenly.

5 Turn down the heat to maintain the temperature at 110°F. Allow a couple more minutes if the whey still looks like milk. Insert the spoon again to check for a break between curds and whey.

CUT GENTLY, DON'T STIR

6 When there is a clear difference in color and texture between the curds and whey, use the whisk (or a knife) to gently slice the larger pieces of curd into (roughly) 1-inch pieces (the distance between the whisk wires will work—do not actually whisk the curd).

7 Remove the pot from the heat and allow the cut curds to rest for 15 minutes.

8 While you wait, line the colander with cheesecloth. Place a bowl (or spare pot) under the colander if you want to collect the whey (see "Uses for One-Hour Whey," page 31); otherwise, place the lined colander in your clean sink.

11 Microwave the curds for 2 minutes on high. Stir them for 25 seconds after heating (no need to get out the stopwatch, just count one haloumi, two haloumi, three haloumi . . .).

NO MICROWAVE?

No problem. Place the pot back on the burner at medium heat and follow the instructions for the stovetop heating method starting on page 107, steps 10–14. Return to this recipe at step 15 on page 98.

9 Gently move the pieces of curd around in the pot, about 2 minutes, to assist the curds as they shrink in the warm whey.

CLOSE-UP

Look for soft, well-defined curds.

10 Pour the entire contents of the pot (curds and whey) into the microwave-safe bowl. The curds will look soft, but well-defined.

CAREFUL, HOT!

12 Microwave the curds again for 2 minutes. Stir thoroughly for a few seconds, and carefully pinch some curds to see if they feel a bit springy.

13 Microwave one last time for 1 minute. This time, press the curds against the sides of the bowl to squeeze out any excess whey until you are confident that there is no unsqueezed curd remaining.

14 If squishing the curd against the bowl is awkward for you, and your hands can handle the heat, squeeze the curd on the spoon a spoonful at a time instead.

15 Pour the curds and whey into the cloth-lined colander and allow the whey to drain completely, about 2 to 5 minutes.

18 . . . and oregano, and mix thoroughly.

19 Gather the corners of the cheesecloth, and twist them together to create a bundle.

16 Press the curd into the colander to squeeze out any remaining whey.

DO YOU DETECT A THEME? YES, WHEY!

17 Add the salt . . .

20 Squeeze the bundle of curd to release even more whey through the colander.

21 Unwrap the curd from the cheesecloth and transfer it to a small loaf pan or other improvised mold for shaping and cooling.

22 Use the spoon to press the cheese firmly down and into the corners of the loaf pan.

23 Cool the cheese in the freezer for 5 to 15 minutes before slicing it or transferring it from the pan.

24 Slice up the cheese and eat it fresh or grilled! Or, if you don't need it right away, let it chill in the refrigerator overnight, which makes it even better for grilling.

VARIATIONS + SUBSTITUTIONS

- Use 100% cow's milk for a milder version.

- Substitute fresh or dried thyme, sumac, or red pepper flakes in place of the oregano for a variety of tangy and piquant Mediterranean flavors.

- Press warm curd into cupcake tins for personal-size cheeses you can warm up on the grill or in a skillet.

GRILLED EGGPLANT ROLLS

— SERVES 4 —

Move over, frozen veggie burgers! You will have some grateful vegetarians at your next barbecue with these on the grill. That said, these rolls are satisfying for everyone, so make plenty: There's nothing worse than the omnivores eating up all the vegetarian food before everyone is fed. My solution as a greedy omnivore is this: Make enough for everyone!

4 grilled or broiled eggplant slices
   (sliced lengthwise)
Extra-virgin olive oil and pepper to taste
4 Haloumi slices (½ inch thick)
8 mint and/or basil leaves
8 grilled or broiled cherry tomatoes
Salt, optional

Brush the eggplant generously with olive oil, season it, and then grill or broil it alongside the slices of haloumi. Grease the grill to prevent your cheese from sticking and don't turn the cheese until it is crispy (and has visible grill marks) on each side.

Using a slice of grilled eggplant as a base, place a piece of haloumi on one narrow end, top it with fresh mint or basil and grilled cherry tomatoes, and roll it closed. Sprinkle the roll with pepper and more olive oil (easy on the salt, remember that this cheese is already quite salty).

The rolls layer well in a lasagna dish if you want to make them ahead and bake them right before serving. These rolls work with zucchini, too—if your eggplant or zucchini are small you can trade in the "roll" concept for more of a stack.

SMOKY CHEATER

This smoky wheel is my attempt at making a one-hour Cheddar—I KNOW, IMPOSSIBLE, but I had to try! Some call me an overachiever; I say I am curious and optimistic! Even I understand that one can only cheat artisanal aging processes so much. But it doesn't mean that I didn't discover a scrumptiously savory, smoky treat of its own kind.

The golden color of this Smoky Cheater comes from the turmeric and paprika and the mouthwatering savory taste from using *smoked* paprika and smoked salt. Though this creation did not end up as I intended, I didn't omit it because, like many experiments in the kitchen, it turned into another good thing. Its haloumi-like process means that it can be broiled or panfried and it won't exactly melt, but rather crust up and brown deliciously on the outside while softening into a pleasing chewy texture on the inside. Can you see where I'm going with this?

Panfried in some butter or ghee (or nothing at all in a nonstick pan), it makes amazing breadless grilled cheese bites—paired with pickles and some crisp greens, you won't miss the bread at all. For real Cheddar in one hour, I'm afraid you'll still have to drive to your local cheese counter. Till then, enjoy this Cheater!

HOW EASY IS IT?

LEVEL: Easy (Easier) Easiest

READY TO EAT IN: 1 Hour

MAKES: 1½ pounds

BIGGEST PAIN: Getting your hands wet and dirty.

USES: Broiling, frying, grilling, snacking.

RECOMMENDED MILK: Whole cow's milk.

WORTH MENTIONING: The immediate results are those of a farmer-style crumbling cheese. This cheese's recommended serving suggestion requires the additional step of panfrying the cheese.

INGREDIENTS

½ teaspoon turmeric

2 teaspoons smoked paprika

1½ teaspoons smoked salt

1 teaspoon flake salt

½ tablet vegetarian rennet

½ cup dechlorinated water

1 gallon whole cow's milk
   (*not* ultra-pasteurized)

3 tablespoons apple cider vinegar

SUPPLIES

½ teaspoon

1 teaspoon

2 small bowls

½ cup

Large colander or mesh strainer

Fine cheesecloth

Large heat-resistant bowl
   (for whey collection), optional

5-quart stockpot

Large whisk

1 tablespoon

Cooking thermometer

Large mixing spoon

Mini round springform cake pan
   or other mold, optional

Milk gallon jug filled halfway with water
   (for pressing cheese), optional

Small plate (for pressing cheese), optional

1 Combine the turmeric and smoked paprika in a small bowl.

4 Line the colander with cheesecloth. Place a bowl under the colander if you want to collect the whey (see "Uses for One-Hour Whey," page 31); otherwise, place the lined colander in your clean sink.

2 Combine the smoked salt and flake salt in a small bowl.

3 Dissolve the ½ tablet of rennet in the ½ cup of water and set it aside.

5 Pour the gallon of milk into the pot and whisk in the apple cider vinegar.

6 Add the spices, whisk them to combine, and heat on medium to 95°F.

TRIP OUT ON THE COOL SWIRLS, MAN!

CLOSE-UP

It's possible that you'll see chunks floating in the whey versus one large mass of curd, and that's fine.

7 Add the rennet solution and mix it in with 20 quick strokes to incorporate it evenly. Heat to 105°F.

8 Look for coagulation to occur between adding the rennet and the milk reaching 105°F. The curd will pull away from the edge when you gently press the top, and you will see a clear separation between the curd and whey.

11 When the temperature of the curds and whey reaches 120°F, reduce the heat. While maintaining the temperature, use the back of the spoon to begin squeezing the curds against the side of the pot.

12 Pull some of the curd up with your spoon and press it with your fingers to track the changes in texture.

9 Use the whisk or spoon to chop the pieces of curd into, (roughly) 1-inch pieces (do not use a whisking action!). Reach down to cut the curd at the bottom of the pot, too. Allow the cut pieces to cook in the whey for about 2 more minutes. Heat to 115°F.

10 Watch the curds change from a softer yogurt-like texture until they come to resemble a sturdy, scrambled egg texture. Continue to heat, this time to 120°F, moving the curds around slowly but continuously with the spoon as you heat.

13 After you've squeezed all the curds against the side of the pot, turn off the heat, and let the pot sit for 5 minutes, or until the curds hold together when you squeeze them.

14 If they don't quite hold, let the curds sit for another 5 to 10 minutes, stirring every couple of minutes to encourage the release of more whey.

15 Pour the curds and whey into the cheesecloth-lined colander.

16 Allow the whey to drain for 3 minutes or until the curds are almost dry, then firmly press out the last of the whey with clean hands.

19 Gather the edges of the cheesecloth and twist them together, squeezing out the remaining whey.

20 Press the bundle into the mold. Depending on the size of the mold, you may have some curd overflow, which requires the removal of some curd to make it fit. In that case, split your curds and make two smaller wheels.

THIS IS CALLED "MILLING" IN THE CHEESEMAKING WORLD.

17 Now break apart the pressed curd with your fingers until it all looks like popcorn.

18 Mix in the salts and stir very thoroughly—dig deep to get that bottom layer!

21 If there's just a small overflow, press to condense the cheese into the mold and to create an even texture.

BEHOLD THE GOLDEN WHEEL!

22 Place the mold in the freezer for 5 minutes. The curd should compress into a wheel in that time. If it still looks crumbly, it may have dried out and cooled off a little too much when you were milling and salting.

ONE-HOUR CHEESE RECIPES: SMOKY CHEATER   **109**

23 More pressing will help: Rewrap the cheese, fill the gallon jug halfway with water and use it as a weight (place a small plate or container on the cheese for a nice flat top). After 10 minutes, let the cheese cool in the freezer for another 5 minutes.

24 Unwrap the cheese and remove it from the mold. Take a cheese knife and dig in! It's very tasty when eaten fresh (use it like Chivo Fresco, page 75) but it really shines when fried in butter.

VARIATIONS + SUBSTITUTIONS

- Use low-fat milk for a firmer texture or raw goat's milk for a tangy undertone. (Note: The yield and creamy texture will decrease a bit with these milk options.)

- Skip the spices and smoked salt, and use 3 teaspoons of flake salt for what I call a Fakin' Feta!

- Add your choice of spices or dried herbs for custom grilled cheese bites.

- Don't shape or cool at all, and use as crumbles for a farmer-style cheese.

GRILLED CHEESE SAMMIES

— MAKES 4 SMALL SANDWICHES —

As I mentioned previously, Cheater became not only a keeper but also a new favorite in my household because of this serving suggestion. If you love a good grilled cheese sandwich, you will love these sammies; they are every bit as familiar and comforting to snack on or to have alongside some tomato soup. These chewy morsels are crusty and addictive right out of the frying pan but all the sandwich fixings make them a proper meal.

¼ batch of Smoky Cheater

2 to 4 tablespoons butter (page 236) or ghee (page 240)

4 to 6 crisp lettuce leaves and thinly sliced pickles to taste

Crispy bacon strips, cucumbers, and other vegetables, optional

Slice the Smoky Cheater into 8 to 12 pieces the size of mini toasts (about 2½ inches by 2½ inches). Melt a teaspoon of butter or ghee onto a hot cast-iron skillet. Fry the cheese slices on medium-high heat until they get toasty brown on both sides. Try flattening them with a spatula to make them ooze a little (like haloumi or paneer, they will not melt but they will get tender and chewy). Pat them with a paper towel if necessary, then stack the toasty sammies with pickles and lettuce leaves, and repeat—as high as you can go.

Slices of bacon don't hurt this combination one bit. Cucumbers are great, but pickled beets, green beans, and even asparagus are tasty, too.

ALE-WASHED SQUEAKIES

I didn't grow up with curds. I had never tasted them until about three years ago when I tried my local Rogue Creamery Cheese Shop's jalapeño version. I simply hadn't come across them growing up in my border town of San Ysidro, California—and because I make cheese and encounter plain curds all the time, they just sounded bland and weird when I finally did hear about them. Thankfully, my conversion was swift and delicious.

If you're not familiar with curds either, I recommend thinking of them as popcorn or chips: Have fun spicing them up with herbs, spices, and infused salts. It's great when a cheese not only tastes good, but *sounds* good, too: This recipe makes for an especially squeaky bite (that kids love), and they're incredibly fun to make. Prepare a couple of batches of plain curds and let everyone customize a handful to their taste: Black pepper and lemon salt or cinnamon and sugar? Why not?

Note: The ale ice bath is a nod to some fancy beer-washed cheeses that I enjoy, and adds a nice layer of complexity to the cheese, but if you want the squeakies to be more kid-friendly, substitute ice water for the ale.

HOW EASY IS IT?

LEVEL: (Easy) Easier Easiest

READY TO EAT IN: 1 hour

MAKES: Just under 1 pound

BIGGEST PAIN: Reheating the whey for the hot whey bath which takes time.

USES: Snacks, replacement for pasta and gnocchi.

RECOMMENDED MILK: 1 gallon low-fat cow's milk (flexible; see variations).

WORTH MENTIONING: Ale/beer is not required for the icy bath—cold wine or plain water work great, too.

INGREDIENTS

½ tablet vegetarian rennet

½ cup dechlorinated water

1 gallon low-fat cow's milk
(*not* ultra-pasteurized)

3 tablespoons lemon juice

16 ounces cold ale

2 cups ice cubes

1 teaspoon flake salt or to taste

1 teaspoon dry or fresh dill

½ teaspoon white pepper

SUPPLIES

½ cup

Large colander or mesh strainer

Fine cheesecloth

Large heat-resistant bowl
(for whey collection), optional

5-quart stockpot

Large whisk

1 tablespoon

Cooking thermometer

Knife

Large mixing spoon

Large slotted spoon or wire spider

Large bowl for ice bath

Paper towels

Large bowl (for drying curds), optional

1 teaspoon

½ teaspoon

1 Dissolve the ½ tablet of rennet in the ½ cup of water and set aside.

4 Heat the milk, on medium, to 95°F.

2 Line the colander with cheesecloth. Place a bowl underneath if you want to collect the whey (see "Uses for One-Hour Whey," page 31); otherwise, place the lined colander in your clean sink.

3 Pour the milk into the pot and whisk or stir in the lemon juice.

5 Add the rennet solution and mix it in with 20 strokes to make sure it is incorporated evenly.

6 Continue to heat the milk, on medium, to 110°F so that the rennet is activated and coagulation occurs.

CLOSE-UP

Don't worry if your pot of milk looks less solid—as long as you see a separation between the curds and whey, you're good.

7 You should have a full pot of curd that looks like yogurt, or you could have many pieces of yogurtlike curd floating in whey—both are great coagulation results.

8 Use a knife to chop the curd into 1-inch chunks. If the entire pot of milk is semisolid, cut the curd by making slices vertically and horizontally, tic-tac-toe style.

11 Lower the heat to maintain the temperature at 115°F. Check that all of the curds have changed from the yogurt texture to a scrambled egg texture. They will look more rounded (having lost their sliced edges) and will not dissolve as easily when pinched.

12 Spoon the curds with a slotted spoon or wire spider into the cheesecloth-lined colander and allow the whey to drain for a few minutes.

9 Then slice at an angle to chop all the way down to the bottom of the pot so that if you had X-ray vision, you would see 1-inch cubes of curd floating in whey.

10 Gently move the pieces of curd around while continuing to heat them to 115°F. The curds will release more whey and shrink as they cook in the hot whey.

13 Use your hands to flatten and press the curds into a slab. You can fold it or flip it over a couple of times to release more whey.

14 Use your hands (or a knife) to break (or cut) the whole slab into snack-size pieces, and set them aside for a few minutes to release a bit more whey.

15 Reheat the whey to 165°F. Gently and without breaking them apart any further, drop the curds into the hot whey. Heat the curds for 5 to 10 minutes, stirring very little, and monitoring the heat to keep it at 165°F.

16 Prep the cold ale bath while the curds heat: Place the ice in the bowl, pour the bottle of ale over the ice, and stir to chill evenly.

19 Spoon the curds into a paper towel–lined bowl to drain, about 2 minutes.

20 Blot the curds dry.

17 After the curds are heated, cold-shock them by spooning them into the ale bath using the slotted spoon or wire spider.

18 Move the curds around in the ale bath until they are completely cool. Pinch and taste them. The texture should be very springy and you will feel a squeak on your teeth when you bite into one.

21 Remove the paper towels from the curds.

22 Add the salt . . .

23 . . . and the dill and pepper.

24 Toss the curds until they're coated evenly.

25 The Ale-Washed Squeakies are complete. Grab another bottle of that ale and turn on a movie!

• You can use whole cow's milk for a richer, softer curd; it will taste delicious, but won't squeak as much.

• Infuse the curds with flavor by adding spices or herbs to the milk while it heats. If they're large herbs, just remember to remove them before adding the rennet. (The coagulation will trap them in a weird way.)

• Experiment with flavor selections; dill and pepper are just one combination of many. What potato chips, flavored popcorn, or nuts do you enjoy? Use those flavors as inspiration!

SQUEAKY "PASTA" PRIMAVERA

— SERVES 2 —

Use your Squeakies as a pasta replacement! With so many people avoiding gluten these days, this recipe will be handy, and it's a delicious change even if you eat traditional pasta. You can make a special batch or use leftover Squeakies, the flavorings of which will likely be hidden by the add-in variations below.

1 cup Ale-Washed Squeakies

1 cup any of the following add-ins to taste: cooked artichoke hearts, black olives, roasted garlic, crisp or roasted sweet red peppers

1 cup marinara sauce, optional

1 tablespoon pesto or shredded basil leaves, optional

Grated Parmigiano Reggiano to taste, optional

Toss the Squeakies with the add-ins, to taste. Eat cold or warm them up in a pan and you're ready to go. But if you'd rather sauce them a little bit, top everything with warm marinara, basil pesto, and grated Parmigiano Reggiano.

Alternatively, the Squeakies also make good "gnocchi," served with brown butter, garlic, and sautéed mushrooms!

FARM-FRESH ROUNDS

Some store-bought cheeses that are labeled "raw" do not completely qualify for that designation, because though they are made from raw (i.e., unpasteurized) milk, they are heated above 115°F, the highest temperature that a food can be heated to maintain raw status. Plus, heating milk above 115°F, whether before or during the cheesemaking process, kills off many of the enzymes and bacteria that make raw milk so flavorful and nutrient-rich (for more on raw or unpasteurized milk, see page 24). I was intrigued by the idea of making a truly raw cheese so that I could fully enjoy the benefits of raw milk.

If you add an acid to warmed (near the cow's body temperature) raw milk, it results in a quick and tender farmers'-style cheese, like this one, that truly demonstrates how much easier it is to make cheese with fresh milk!

This cheese gets its tang from the lemon juice, which just adds to the ultra-fresh flavor. It melts well, and though you lose some of the live enzymes when that happens, it's nice to have that option with such a fast process. It's so fast that you can easily make and eat this entire batch all within a half hour. Yes, I said *and* eat!

HOW EASY IS IT?

LEVEL: Easy   Easier   Easiest

READY TO EAT IN: 20 minutes

MAKES: 4 to 6 ounces

BIGGEST PAIN: The low-heat process results in a small yield. (Tip! See Uses for One-Hour Whey, page 31, to make use of this extra-rich whey.)

USES: Eat raw or melt on pizza, roasted veggies, or enchiladas.

RECOMMENDED MILK: Raw whole cow's milk.

WORTH MENTIONING: You may not need the extra 3 tablespoons of lemon juice.

INGREDIENTS

½ gallon raw whole cow's milk
(*not* ultra-pasteurized)

1 tablespoon flake salt

½ cup plus 3 tablespoons lemon juice,
freshly squeezed and strained of pulp

SUPPLIES

3-quart stockpot

1 tablespoon

Cooking thermometer

½ cup

Large mixing spoon

Gloves, optional

1 Pour the milk into the pot.

4 Pour the ½ cup of lemon juice into the pot
(reserve the additional 3 tablespoons) and stir
thoroughly as you heat the milk to 110°F.

2 Add the salt to the milk and stir it well so it dissolves.

3 Heat the salty milk on low to medium heat until it reaches 105°F.

TIP! Some people prefer to steer clear of fresh citrus juice for cheesemaking because the acidity varies so much. While that's true, if you squeeze more than you need when you're prepping your ingredients, you can stop pouring in the juice when you see coagulation. If you need a bit more, add 1 tablespoon at a time. If you find that you went too far and your cheese feels a little dry, adjust the lemon juice next time.

JUICY TIDBIT.

COAGULATION!

5 The curd will start to form into waves, with a texture resembling a poached egg. If you see no separation between curds and whey, add the extra lemon juice one tablespoon at a time, stirring and waiting 30 seconds for clear curd formation.

NOTE: If you have sensitive hands, wear gloves or use a spoon.

6 As soon as you see coagulation, turn off the heat. Confirm that the temperature has not risen and carefully dip your clean hands into the pot to gather and press the curd into (roughly) 3-inch rounds.

7 Gently press out the remaining whey while forming the cheese into rustic mini-rounds (think plump patties). Applying light pressure will yield tender slices. Firm pressure will result in moist crumbles.

8 You should be able to shape about three 3-inch rounds. That's it! Your Farm-Fresh Rounds are ready to slice or crumble onto your favorite dish.

VARIATIONS + SUBSTITUTIONS

- Sprinkle the rounds with dry or fresh herbs, cracked pepper, or chili pepper flakes immediately after shaping.

- Store the rounds in herbed olive oil in a glass jar.

- Shape into one large wheel, or no wheel at all, and break up for crumbles.

RAW DEAL PIZZA STACK

— MAKES 2 STACKS; SERVES 2 —

What's the deal? We're making everyone's favorite snack in two minutes. Experiment and stack anything you would normally like on your pizza that you also enjoy raw. You can, of course, just use this cheese on regular pizza as a fast and delicious melty cheese.

4 "crusts" (choice of sliced tomato, olive oil–marinated eggplant round, or a pineapple slice)

4 thick slices or generous crumbles of Farm-Fresh Rounds

½ cup of choice of toppings (fresh basil, sliced spinach, sliced red peppers, olives, and/or fresh or marinated mushrooms)

2 tablespoons of choice of "sauce" (sun-dried tomatoes in olive oil, pesto, olive tapenade, and/ or drizzle of olive oil, and salt/ pepper/oregano)

Start each stack with your "crust" of choice at the bottom. Top each crust with a slice of cheese, follow with the toppings, and then repeat. Finally, spoon the sauce over everything. My favorite Pizza Stack is a tomato slice crust, Farm-Fresh Round crumbles, coarse black pepper, sliced Kalamata olives, and basil pesto drizzled over everything. Yum.

TRIPLE PEPPER HACK

Triple Pepper Hack is my love letter to Monterey Jack, which, when I ate it in quesadillas almost daily as a kid, I assumed was a Mexican cheese. It turns out it was not created in Mexico, though it does have California roots and some ties to Spanish monks, too. One of the many colorful definitions of the word *hack* is "unauthorized access or programming in a wizardly fashion," and though this Triple Pepper Hack may be an unauthorized creation, if you like nachos (who doesn't?) and a bit of wizardry (again, who doesn't?), you'll be so excited to have this cheese in your skill box. The process is not that of a true Monterey Jack (which is traditionally aged for one to four months), but I hacked and merged a few more standard recipes so that you can enjoy something similar within an hour. You can cast your own spells and customize this one to fit your taste—add more spicy peppers, leave it plain, or add mild roasted green and red peppers. Quintuple Pepper Hack, anyone?

HOW EASY IS IT?

LEVEL: Easy   Easier   (Easiest)

READY TO EAT IN: 45 minutes

MAKES: 1½ pounds

BIGGEST PAIN: Making sure you don't touch the peppers—and then your eyes—with your bare hands. Wearing gloves is not a bad idea!

USES: Great snack on its own and great shredded onto nachos, quesadillas, frittatas, tacos, or baked potatoes,

RECOMMENDED MILK: Whole cow's milk, 1 cup plain yogurt (flexible, see variations).

WORTH MENTIONING: This recipe relies on microwave use; alternate instructions for heating and stretching are included, but may take longer.

INGREDIENTS

1½ teaspoons citric acid

½ cup plus ¼ cup dechlorinated water

¼ tablet vegetarian rennet

1 cup plain yogurt, any fat content

1 gallon whole cow's milk
(*not* ultra-pasteurized)

2 tablespoons pickled jalapeño peppers,
diced (like the ones used on nachos)

1 tablespoon chili pepper flakes

1 teaspoon coarse or cracked
black pepper

2 teaspoons flake salt

SUPPLIES

1 teaspoon

½ teaspoon

½ cup

¼ cup

1 cup

Large whisk, optional

5-quart stockpot

Large mixing spoon

Cooking thermometer

Large slotted spoon, optional

Large microwave-safe bowl

1 tablespoon

Plastic gloves, optional

Small loaf pan or other cheese mold

Parchment or waxed paper

1 Stir the citric acid into the ½ cup of water and set it aside.

4 Pour the milk into the pot and whisk the yogurt in thoroughly.

2 Dissolve the ¼ tablet of rennet in the ¼ cup of water and set it aside.

A WHISK HELPS!

3 Stir the cup of yogurt so that it will incorporate into the milk more easily.

5 Stir in the citric acid solution and heat the milk on medium to 90°F.

6 When the milk temperature reaches 90°F, add the rennet solution. Mix it in with 20 quick strokes to make sure it incorporates evenly. Then, without stirring, continue heating to 105°F if you will be using a microwave to stretch the cheese (if not, heat to 110°F).

TIP! Always take temperature readings from several parts of the pot, since some areas in the pot may be hotter than others. The milk reaches the ideal temperature quickly, so stay close. You will start to see a clear separation between curds and whey, significant clumps, or a consistent yogurt-like texture.

7 When the milk reaches 105°F (or 110°F), lower the heat to maintain that temperature and use a spoon to cut any large clumps of curd into 1- to 2-inch pieces. Slowly move the pieces around the pot to help shrink them as they cook in the warm whey.

NO MICROWAVE?

No problem. Follow the "Hot Whey Bath Instructions" on page 144, starting with step 1.

10 Microwave the curds for 1 minute on high (the default quick-heat settings usually do the trick). Fold the curd mass over itself 5 times to distribute the heat evenly. Drain off any whey that is released. Microwave for 30 seconds on the same setting.

11 Drain the whey immediately and sprinkle the peppers, pepper flakes, black pepper, and salt on the curds.

8 When the texture of the curds has changed from that of soft yogurt to that of a scrambled egg, scoop the curds into the microwave-safe bowl. (It's okay if a couple of pieces still look like yogurt.)

9 Drain any visible whey into the pot as you hold the curds with your hands or a spoon.

IT'S STARTING TO LOOK YUMMY!

12 Fold the curds over the peppers 10 times to incorporate them evenly. (Note: The curds are starting to get very hot, so use a spoon or clean plastic gloves instead of bare hands.) The curds should be more uniform in texture now.

13 Microwave for another 30 seconds. There should be little whey now. Fold and knead to distribute the heat evenly. The curd may come together in as few as 5 folds or as many as 30. (It depends on milk type and curd temperature.)

CLOSE-UP

The curds will start out lumpy, but in a couple of minutes, you will see their transformation into a neat, springy mass.

14 Shape your Triple Pepper Hack into a standard loaf (see page 184 for other options) by lining a pan with parchment paper (so it releases easily) and pressing the hot curd into it.

15 Put the cheese in the freezer for 5 to 10 minutes to cool. Then lift the paper out of the pan, remove the cheese, and flip it for smooth presentation.

YOUR WORK HERE IS DONE. SNACK TIME HAS JUST BEGUN!

VARIATIONS + SUBSTITUTIONS

- Skip the yogurt: It's not necessary for coagulation, but it adds a nice tang to the cheese. If you do use it, any fat content will work.

- Use low-fat milk instead of whole milk for a firm texture similar to string cheese; or try it with raw goat's milk to up the tang factor well beyond the yogurt contribution.

- Omit or replace any or all peppers and invent your own creation (diced olives and salami, currants and rosemary?). Make a new version every week!

- Shape the Jack Hack into round bowls, flat circles, or hand-shaped loaves.

QUESADILLAS 2.0

— MAKES 2 QUESADILLAS; SERVES 2 —

Don't get me wrong: I've rarely met a quesadilla I didn't devour. But this is truly a crave-worthy version: It's so, so much more than a chewy white flour tortilla stuffed with yellow cheese. A tiny bit of effort and the right ingredients will amplify the experience for you, too. Lazy?—ahem, I mean—short on time? Use premade corn tortillas! Just sprinkle your store-bought corn tortillas with water before heating on a skillet for a much fresher flavor.

- 4 corn tortillas or ½ cup masa harina
- ½ cup shredded or sliced Triple Pepper Hack
- 4 teaspoons ghee (page 240) or butter (page 236)

FOR HOMEMADE TORTILLAS: Follow package directions to form small balls of dough about as big as Ping-Pong balls and pat them down (unless you have a tortilla press, of course) into (roughly) ⅛-inch-thick tortillas.

FOR THE QUESADILLAS: Place half of the cheese all over one tortilla and cover it with the other tortilla to make a sandwich. If using masa, press the edges down to contain your cheese. Fry the quesadilla in ghee in a hot cast-iron skillet, flipping it midway, until the masa is cooked and crispy on both sides and the cheese is melted inside, about one minute per side. It should be crunchy on the outside, melty on the inside. Repeat. Now tell me that isn't something special.

FAVORITE MELTY MOZZARELLA

To make this classic cheese super-easy for you to whip up, I've cut the recipe down to the essentials: The use of a microwave allows for a hassle-free and consistent heating method that helps in the stretching process characteristic of a pasta filata, or "pulled ribbon"–style cheese. The citric acid allows the rennet to do its job without you having to wait a day to let the milk acidify with cultures. This Favorite Melty Mozzarella is so tender and versatile, you will find yourself making it often and for dishes beyond pizza. Keep it simple, and shape it into large mozzarella balls, make many little mouthfuls (bocconcini, page 192), or braid it—you can flavor it, slice it, shred it, fill it, roll it flat, and pinwheel it! (See all of the pulled curd shaping techniques on page 192–198.) The point is, this basic recipe is just the beginning. And though the stretching takes a little practice, the flavor is what matters. As you practice, you may end up with some funny-shaped cheese along the way, but you'll love every delicious minute of it!

HOW EASY IS IT?

LEVEL: Easy (Easier) Easiest

READY TO EAT IN: 45 minutes

MAKES: 1½ pounds

BIGGEST PAIN: Pasteurization varies and ultra-pasteurized milk (sometimes unlabeled) does not allow coagulation with this recipe.

USES: Your go-to snacking and melting cheese for everything.

RECOMMENDED MILK: 1 gallon whole cow's milk, and 1 cup cow's milk cream—also called heavy cream or whipping cream (flexible, if desired; see variations).

WORTH MENTIONING: This recipe relies on microwave use; alternate instructions for heating and stretching are included, but may take longer and require more practice.

INGREDIENTS

1½ teaspoons citric acid

½ cup plus ¼ cup dechlorinated water

¼ tablet vegetarian rennet

1 gallon whole cow's milk
(*not* ultra-pasteurized)

1 cup cream (*not* ultra-pasteurized),
optional

2 teaspoons flake salt

SUPPLIES

1 teaspoon

½ teaspoon

½ cup

¼ cup

5-quart stockpot

Large slotted spoon

Cooking thermometer

Large microwave-safe casserole dish
or bowl

Plastic gloves, optional

Parchment or waxed paper, optional

Large bowl (for ice bath), optional

1 Stir the citric acid into the ½ cup water and set aside.

CLOSE-UP

You may see some slight coagulation when you add the citric acid—there's more to come!

4 Stir in the well-dissolved citric acid solution and heat on medium to 90°F.

2 Dissolve the ¼ tablet of rennet in the ¼ cup of water and set it aside.

3 Pour the milk into the pot. Optional: Add the cup of cream to make a more succulent cheese, closer to fresh mozzarella di bufala!

NICE COAGULATION!

5 When the milk temperature reaches 90°F, add the rennet solution and mix it in with 20 quick strokes to make sure it is incorporated evenly. Then, without stirring, continue heating.

6 Heat to 105°F if you plan on using the microwave method to stretch the cheese (for stretching in a hot whey bath, heat to 110°F). Coagulation will start to happen; look for separation between curds and whey, clumps, or a yogurt-like texture.

7 Use the spoon to slice large clumps of curd to just 1 to 2 inches in size. Slowly move the pieces around in the warm whey for 1 minute to help them shrink as they cook. Lower the heat to hold the temperature of the milk as soon as it reaches 105°F/110°F.

8 When the texture of the curds has changed from that of soft yogurt to that of a scrambled egg (about 2 additional minutes of cooking and gentle stirring), scoop the curds into the microwave-safe bowl.

NO MICROWAVE?

No problem. Follow the "Hot Whey Bath Instructions" on page 144, starting with step 1.

11 Microwave again for 30 seconds on high. Drain the whey immediately. Sprinkle salt on the curds and fold and flatten them 10 times to incorporate the salt evenly. (Note: If it's too hot on your hands, use a spoon or wear clean plastic gloves.)

QUICK, QUICK, YOUR CURDS ARE COOLING!

9 Drain off any visible whey into the pot as you hold the curds with your hands or a spoon. Flatten the curds across the bowl for more even heating.

10 Microwave the curds for 1 minute on high (the default quick-heat settings usually do the trick). Using the spoon or your hands, fold the curd mass over itself 5 times, to distribute the heat evenly. Drain off any whey that is released.

12 Microwave for another 30 seconds on high. There should be very little whey now. Fold the curds over themselves repeatedly, pressing down between folds. The curds normally transform most dramatically into cheese after this heating.

13 The curd temperature should be 135°F, though you don't want to stop to check, since the curds will cool in the time it takes to do so. The curds may come together to form one large mass in as few as 5 folds or as many as 30.

14 During the folding process, the curds will start out looking a little like lumpy cookie batter, then will suddenly become springy and stretchy like perfect bread dough. Test it by stretching the curd a little every few folds.

15 The curd becomes mozzarella when the edges look smooth and the surface looks shiny when stretched. This is when you can form it into smooth balls, ropes, or other shapes.

CAN YOU
BELIEVE IT?
SO GOOD, RIGHT? ↱

VARIATIONS + SUBSTITUTIONS

- Try low-fat cow's milk—the sturdy result will be easier to shred—or try raw goat's milk for a tangy flavor (pasteurized goat's milk curd is not very sturdy). Beware, however, the texture will not be as creamy, and the yield will decrease a bit with these alternate milks.

- Add herbs, cracked black pepper, chili pepper flakes, and anything from bacon crumbles to dried fruit bits when you add and fold the salt into the curd.

- See Chapter 3, Shapes and Flavors (page 182), for some really fun ways to shape your cheese. (Hint: Cheese ravioli will take on a whole new meaning!)

16 If you like the result now, you are done. If the curd tears or shreds into strings, it cooled too much for additional stretching. Heat it in the microwave for another 30 seconds. (Note: The less you heat and stretch your mozzarella, the more tender it will be.)

KEBAB PARTY

— MAKES 6 KEBABS; SERVES 6 —

Prepare the raw kebabs in advance, or better yet, put all of the components and skewers out for a DIY raw kebab party. You can sit back and supervise. Insist on taste-testing, of course!

20 to 25 cubes of Favorite Melty Mozzarella (1 inch x 1 inch)

1½ tablespoons olive oil

1½ tablespoons red wine vinegar

salt and pepper to taste

20 to 25 cherry tomatoes, sweet pepper pieces, pitted olives, and/or basil leaves

6 skewer sticks

Toss the cubes of mozzarella in the olive oil, vinegar, salt, and pepper. Alternate 4 to 5 cubes of mozzarella with 4 to 5 of your chosen goodies on each skewer. This idea works with fruit, too—use tiny skewers for party appetizers or long ones for a picnic side-salad-on-a-stick!

Hot Whey Bath Instructions

You can avoid using a microwave for the cheeses in the Melty and Gooey section; it simply takes a little more practice to stretch the curd in hot whey. You can easily shape the curd into balls or other basic shapes; stretching into ropes is more challenging, because getting the curd hot enough without losing tenderness is tricky. The results are delicious and it is quite handy to learn this method in the event that you are in the woods making cheese . . . or just don't want to use a microwave. Choose tender cheese versus a long stretchy curd and you'll enjoy this traditional method!

INGREDIENTS

Prepared curd

Remaining whey

2 tablespoons plus ¼ teaspoon
flake salt

SUPPLIES

Cooking thermometer

1 tablespoon

Large whisk

Large heat-resistant bowl

Ladle or large spoon

Thick plastic dishwashing gloves,
optional

Smaller spoon, optional

¼ teaspoon

1 After removing the curds from the whey, continue heating the whey to 190°F. Once the whey reaches that temperature, lower the heat or turn it off to maintain the temperature. You can turn the stove back on and heat later if necessary.

2 Add the 2 tablespoons of salt to the hot whey and stir well to dissolve (this causes it to turn a milkier color).

3 Split the curd into 4 portions and set 3 aside. Place 1 portion into another heat-resistant bowl—the curd may not hold together completely, and that's okay. Do your best to hold it together.

4 Ladle enough hot whey from the pot into the bowl to cover the single portion of curd. Allow the curd to soften for about 3 minutes in the hot whey. The curd has to reach about 135°F to 145°F in order for you to be able to knead it properly.

HANDS
OR SPOONS!

5 Using your hands—gloved or not—or a spoon and a ladle (the whey is very hot so be careful with bare hands), start to shape the curd into one mass.

6 Even the core should feel softer—if it doesn't, let the curd sit longer in the whey. Use a thermometer to test the temperature, but eventually teach yourself to go by feel, because the curd will actually cool several important degrees while you test.

9 Repeat steps 3–8 with the remaining 3 curd portions. (Try cutting the curd into smaller cubes so that it heats faster—which also allows you to practice on many small mozzarella balls.)

10 You will see improvement with each portion you try. As you start to get the hang of this method, try working with half of the curd. (If you're comparing processes, though, do not expect the same stretch that is possible with microwave heating.)

7 Keeping the softened curd submerged in the hot whey, fold it onto itself 3 to 5 times so that you can easily grab it as one mass and lift it out of the whey. The curd texture will become smoother and more springy, and will look shinier.

8 Taste a pinch of the curd. If needed, sprinkle on ¼ teaspoon of the remaining salt and quickly fold it 5 more times in your hands (out of the whey) to incorporate the salt and form a ball. Repeat steps 6 and 7 if necessary.

CHEESE FOLKLORE!

Legend has it that the hot whey bath used in the cheesemaking process was originally made with hot sea water—and that the mozzarella was seasoned with that salt alone! . . . Not that I'm planning on trying that with a pot of the Pacific Ocean any time soon.

Shaping Mozzarella

There are 2 ways I like to shape mozzarella—one way is simple and no-fuss and the other gives you more control over the shape of the finished cheese. The easiest way (right) to shape warm mozzarella is to let it take the shape of whatever bowl you cool it in.

The ice bath method (below) is more about preserving a shape you have created. By cooling it quickly, you can "freeze" the cheese into shape.

1 Line the bowl with parchment or waxed paper (optional). Place the bowl in the freezer for 5 minutes to help cool and shape the cheese quickly.

METHOD 2: ICE BATH

1 Fill a bowl about three-quarters full with cold water, then top it off with ice cubes. Roll out a piece of parchment or waxed paper, and place the warm mozzarella ball in the center. (See box for mini balls, braids, etc.)

2 Wrap up the cheese, rolling it in the paper, then twist the paper ends tightly at each end. The shape of your bundle will predict the shape of your cheese.

2 A small, round bowl is handy and, when inverted, makes for a cute, loafy, dome shape for the cheese!

MOZZARELLA, UNWRAPPED

When using Method 2, below, note that mini balls, braids, and knots can all be dunked directly in the ice without any wrapping. And since some salt will naturally be lost in the water, do not allow the mozzarella to sit in the ice bath longer than 2 minutes, or add more salt during the heating process to compensate.

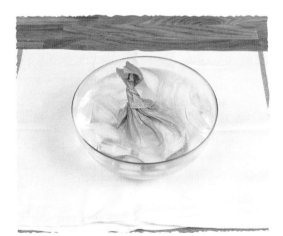

3 Place the bundle in the ice bath. The mozzarella will seize up immediately, but 2 to 4 minutes longer should be sufficient for the cheese to cool if you plan to eat the cheese right away. Ice a few minutes longer if you plan to store it for later.

4 Pull the bundle from the bath, and unwrap the shaped mozzarella! It's ready to eat or store in a covered container. If any water leaked into the bundle, simply blot dry with a paper towel or clean cheesecloth.

PIZZA FILATA

This cheese gets its name from the familiar flavors I chose and the process involved in making string cheese. The hot curd for a *pasta filata*–style cheese is pulled into ribbons (the direct translation for pasta filata is "spun paste"—not as appetizing as "pulled ribbons" is it?) in the same manner as mozzarella (see page 137), Oaxaca (see page 161), and other chewy cheeses from around the world. By folding the curd ribbons over and over themselves like taffy, you get thin layers of cheese that can be pulled off individually—which is how we end up with string cheese!

With this style cheese, the use of low-fat milk is important, since it's the difference between ending up with a cheese known for its creaminess and one known for its stringiness. We're aiming for the latter.

Pizza filata is a crowd pleaser: It's an incredibly fun cheese for kids—from making it, to stripping it apart, to chowing down one chewy piece at a time. There's something about interactive food that is intriguing no matter your age. You can make grown-up string cheese for your next dinner party and doctor it up with fancy add-ins, like fresh rosemary and rainbow cracked pepper, anise seeds and dried cranberries, crunchy pink salt and fresh lemon thyme . . . oh, the possibilities!

HOW EASY IS IT?

LEVEL: (Easy) Easier Easiest

READY TO EAT IN: 1 hour

MAKES: 1½ pounds

BIGGEST PAIN: Not getting a great stretch as you learn; it does take some practice to get the heat just right.

USES: Serious snacking and bragging at school or work; use like part-skim mozzarella.

RECOMMENDED MILK: Low-fat cow's milk.

WORTH MENTIONING: This recipe relies on microwave use; alternate instructions for heating and stretching are provided, but may take longer and will yield balls of cheese or short ropes.

INGREDIENTS

1½ teaspoons citric acid

½ cup plus ¼ cup dechlorinated water

¼ tablet vegetarian rennet

1 gallon low-fat cow's milk
(*not* ultra-pasteurized)

2 teaspoons flake salt

1 teaspoon dried oregano or Italian herb
blend

2 teaspoons sun-dried tomatoes, diced
(not in oil)

SUPPLIES

1 teaspoon

½ teaspoon

½ cup

¼ cup

5-quart stockpot

Large slotted spoon

Cooking thermometer

Large microwave-safe bowl

Large bowl for ice bath

Lint-free tea towel or paper towels

1 Stir the citric acid into the ½ cup of water and set it aside.

4 Heat on medium to 90°F.

2 Dissolve the ¼ tablet of rennet in the ¼ cup of water and set it aside.

3 Pour the milk into the pot, and stir in the citric acid solution.

... 18, 19, 20!

5 At 90°F, add the rennet solution and mix it in with 20 quick strokes to make sure it is incorporated evenly. Continue heating to 105°F if you plan on using the microwave to heat and stretch the cheese (for stretching in a hot whey bath, heat to 110°F).

6 Stay close and monitor the heat. The milk reaches temperature quickly and overheating can ruin the batch. Look for a separation between curds and whey, clumps, or a yogurt-like texture. Lower the heat to hold the temperature of the milk at 105°F (or 110°F).

7 Use the spoon to gently slice through any large clumps of curd so that the largest curds are just 1 to 2 inches. Slowly move the pieces around in the warm whey to help them shrink as they cook.

8 When the texture of the curds has changed from that of soft yogurt to that of a scrambled egg (about 2 minutes), scoop the curds into the microwave-safe bowl.

10 Using the spoon or your hands, fold the curd mass over itself 5 times to distribute the heat evenly. Drain off any whey that was released. Microwave again for 30 seconds and drain the whey immediately.

11 Sprinkle the salt, oregano, and sun-dried tomato bits on the curds, and fold 10 times to incorporate it all evenly.

QUICK, QUICK, YOUR CURDS ARE COOLING!

NO MICROWAVE?

No problem. Follow the "Hot Whey Bath Instructions" on page 144, starting with step 1.

9 Pour any extra whey into the pot as you hold the curds with your hands or a spoon. Spread the curds across the bottom of the bowl for more even heating. Microwave the bowl of curds for 1 minute on high.

NEARLY THERE!

12 As you fold the curds, you will start to notice changes in texture: They will be less lumpy, will be coming together, and will feel a little springy. You may even see signs of melting.

13 Microwave for another 30 seconds. There should be very little whey now. Continue to fold the curds. It will start out looking like cookie batter and transform into a texture more like bread dough.

14 The curd could come together in as few as 5 folds or as many as 30, depending on how hot the curds are and how processed your milk is. When it comes together completely and looks smooth, take it between your hands and try to stretch it.

15 When the curd stretches easily, pull it as long as you can without it breaking.

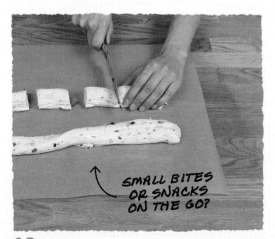

SMALL BITES OR SNACKS ON THE GO?

18 When you are satisfied with the length and thickness of the cheese rope (I aim for about 24 inches of rope, an inch or two in thickness), cut the rope into pieces. The length is entirely up to you—typical string cheese is about 4 inches long.

BRRR!

19 Prepare the ice bath by filling a bowl about three-quarters full with cold water, then adding ice cubes to top it off. Drop the warm Pizza Filata pieces into the ice water for a minute or two so they retain their shape.

The string cheese effect is achieved with the help of low-fat milk and the stretching and folding. The more folds, the thinner the shreds.

16 Then fold the curd over itself before stretching it again. Continue to stretch and fold until you have a long rope of cheese. Four to six stretches are sufficient, but you can keep going with it as long as it's warm and stretchy.

17 If the curd tears, it's a good time to stop. If you'd like to stretch it longer and thinner, heat it for another 30 seconds, and continue to stretch and fold.

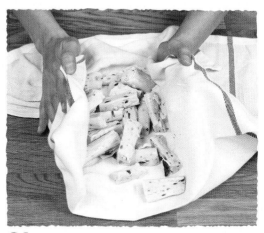

20 Spoon the cheese pieces from the ice bath and place them onto a clean, lint-free towel or paper towel.

21 Gently dry the cheese pieces with the towel.

22 Transfer the cheese pieces to a plate, and you're ready to amaze.

MORE FUN TO PEEL THAN A BANANA!

• Use raw skimmed cow's milk instead of low-fat store-bought milk and use the cream to make butter.

• Add any other tasty bits that you enjoy (see suggestions in the Pizza Filata introduction, page 151) to the curd. Make a couple of varieties out of the same batch.

• Shape the warm curd into doughnut shapes, pretzels, or tight coils . . . or create your own signature knot! Remember to "shock" them into shape in the ice bath.

• Leave the cheese in one superlong rope that you serve across the table on parchment paper, and let your guests tear into it as an appetizer.

SALAMI POCKETS

— MAKES 10 POCKETS; SERVES 2 —

You've had pizza pockets from the frozen-food section and secretly love them, right? Give these a try for a surprising yet familiar (and fast!) treat on a movie night. And I didn't forget you, vegetarian friends: Use panfried slices of zucchini or vegetarian pepperoni slices for equally delicious pockets.

20 slices of salami (Genoa or similar)
¼ cup thick marinara or pizza sauce
5 small Pizza Filata pieces, shredded

Top a slice of salami with a small dollop of marinara sauce, then a few shreds of Pizza Filata, then another slice of salami. Like a sandwich! Make lots of these and either pan-sear them in a dry skillet (the salami will release fat) or bake them on cookie sheets at 350°F until the salami gets crispy and the cheese melts, 10 to 15 minutes.

Vary the filling by inserting a sliced olive, mushroom, baby spinach leaf, or other pizza topping.

Serve with a crisp green salad with vinaigrette for a simple but Friday night–worthy dinner.

CHIPOTLE-LIME OAXACA

Now we drop a pin on the map at Oaxaca, Mexico, for another popular "pulled ribbon"–style cheese (see Pizza Filata, page 151). It's fun to knot the pulled curd as is done traditionally with queso oaxaca (which is, FYI, simply called *quesillo* in Oaxaca) and pull it apart in stringy, snackable chunks, but this cheese doesn't stop there: It can be sliced, shredded, and melted like mozzarella.

This version earns some additional style (and flavor) points when you coat the ribbons with smoky goodness before knotting. Sprinkle them with savory chipotle powder (dried, smoked, and ground red jalapeños) or mix the powder with fresh lime juice (natural pals) for a festive rub. The resulting color of the spice-rubbed cheese is tempting on any table, and the elegant knot makes a stunning appetizer for a dinner party. Serve it up with some ice-cold Mexican beer and tortilla chips for a combo I challenge someone to dislike!

HOW EASY IS IT?

LEVEL: (Easy) Easier Easiest

READY TO EAT IN: 1 hour

MAKES: 1½ pounds

BIGGEST PAIN: It may take some practice before you get the temperature just right for a good stretch.

USES: Ideal for using in Mexican or other Latin dishes, but it can really make scrambled eggs and chili special!

RECOMMENDED MILK: 1 gallon low-fat cow's milk.

WORTH MENTIONING: This recipe relies on microwave use; alternate instructions for heating and stretching are provided (page 144), but may take longer and will result in balls or short ropes instead of a knot.

INGREDIENTS

1½ teaspoons citric acid

½ cup plus ¼ cup dechlorinated water

¼ tablet vegetarian rennet

Juice of 1 lime

2 teaspoons chipotle chili powder

2 teaspoons plus ½ teaspoon flake salt

1 gallon low-fat cow's milk
    (*not* ultra-pasteurized)

1 teaspoon lemon pepper

SUPPLIES

1 teaspoon

½ teaspoon

½ cup

¼ cup

Knife

Citrus juicer

5-quart stockpot

Large slotted spoon

Cooking thermometer

Large microwave-safe bowl

Plastic gloves, optional

Parchment or waxed paper, optional

Large bowl for ice bath

1 Stir the citric acid into the ½ cup of water and set aside.

4 Pour the milk into the pot, and stir in the citric acid solution.

2 Dissolve the ¼ tablet of rennet in the ¼ cup of water and set it aside.

3 Squeeze the lime juice and add it to the chipotle powder and the ½ teaspoon of salt in a small bowl to make the spice rub.

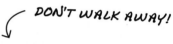
DON'T WALK AWAY!

5 Heat on medium to 90°F, then add the rennet solution and mix it in with 20 quick strokes to make sure it is incorporated evenly. Continue heating to 105°F if you plan on using the microwave to heat and stretch the cheese (for stretching in a hot whey bath, heat to 110°F).

6 Stay close and monitor the heat. The milk will reach temperature quickly, and overheating can ruin the batch. Look for a separation between curds and whey, clumps, or a yogurt-like texture.

7 Lower the heat to hold your temperature at 105°F (or 110°F). Use the spoon to gently slice through any large clumps of curd so the largest curds are just 1 to 2 inches. Slowly move the pieces around to help them shrink as they cook.

8 When the texture of the curds has changed from that of soft yogurt to that of scrambled eggs, scoop the curds into the microwave-safe bowl.

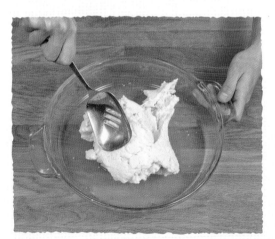

10 Using the spoon or your hands, fold the curd mass over itself 5 times to distribute the heat evenly. Microwave again for 30 seconds. Drain off any whey that is released. Then drain the whey immediately (quickly, your curds are cooling!).

11 Sprinkle the lemon pepper and the remaining 2 teaspoons of salt on the curds and fold 10 times to incorporate it all evenly.

NO MICROWAVE?

No problem. Follow the "Hot Whey Bath Instructions" on page 144, starting with step 1.

9 Pour the extra whey back into the pot as you hold the curds with your hands or a spoon. Spread the curds across the bottom of the bowl for more even heating. Microwave for 1 minute on high (the default quick-heat settings usually do the trick).

12 As you fold the curds, you should start feeling a difference in texture: The curds should be coming together now, and feel a little springy. You may even see little melting strings.

13 Microwave for another 30 seconds. There should be very little whey now. Continue to fold the curds, kneading them aggressively with your hands (use gloves or two spoons if the curd is too hot for your hands). It will start looking like bread dough.

ALMOST THERE!

STRETCH AND FOLD; STREEEETCH, AND FOLD . . .

14 The curd could come together in as few as 5 folds or as many as 30, depending on the milk quality and how hot the curd is. When it all sticks together as one smooth mass, take the curd in your hands and try to stretch it.

15 When the curd stretches easily, pull it as long as you can without breaking it. Fold it over itself and stretch and fold again.

18 To make a knot, simply hold on to one end of the rope with two fingers, and with the other hand, start wrapping the other end of the rope around the end that you are holding.

19 Shift the angles as you wrap down and up, so that you don't end up with a simple spiral.

16 Four to six stretches should be sufficient. (Note: If the curd tears, it's a good time to stop; if you'd like to stretch it longer and thinner, heat it for another 30 seconds, and continue to stretch and fold.)

17 When you are satisfied with the thickness of the cheese rope (aim for about 1 to 2 inches thick), decide if you will make one, two, or three knots. Cut the rope into one piece per knot, and start dipping them into the chipotle-lime rub.

20 Remove the two fingers holding the stationary end of the rope and tuck the end into the reserved spot.

DRIZZLE A LITTLE MORE OF THE CHIPOTLE-LIME RUB ON YOUR KNOT. YUM!

21 This cheese is perfectly scrumptious warm, but if you want to save it for later, or show off a tidy little bundle, wrap the knot or knots in parchment or waxed paper, twisting the top of the paper tightly around the cheese.

22 Prepare an ice bath by filling a bowl about three-quarters full with cold water, then adding ice cubes to top it off. Float the bundles in the bowl of icy water for 3 to 5 minutes, and gently squeeze them to check for firmness.

23 Retrieve the bundles, unwrap the cheese, and it's ready to serve—but don't forget to tear off a piece of this lip-smacking cheese for yourself!

VARIATIONS + SUBSTITUTIONS

- Vary the rub and use lemon juice and ground white pepper or mild chili powder (if the powdered chipotle proves too hard to find, or offers up too much of a kick).

- For basic oaxaca, leave the chili rub out altogether and just sprinkle the ropes lightly with salt before knotting. It is equally delicious!

- Make small oaxaca knots instead of one big one. Or, if the knot gives you trouble, simple twists or grape-size morsels make great small bites, too.

- Skip the knot and just fold the curd over until it holds together. Place it in a bowl or pan to shape it into a wheel (see Smoky Cheater, page 103). Cover the wheel in the rub after it cools.

CUCUMBER RIBBON SALAD

— MAKES 2 SMALL SALADS; SERVES 2 —

Cooling cucumber balances the spicy chipotle and blends perfectly with lime in this simple but scrumptious salad. We shred the cucumber into ribbons to match the oaxaca shreds for a textured treat and stylish look. Enjoy as a snack or side salad.

4-inch piece of Chipotle-Lime Oaxaca cheese

1 peeled cucumber

½ tablespoon freshly squeezed lime juice

¼ teaspoon sea salt or to taste

Pull the oaxaca apart into ribbons or shreds. Using a vegetable peeler, make twice as many cucumber ribbons as cheese, then toss both with the lime juice and a sprinkling of sea salt (adjust to taste).

If you are left with any excess chipotle-lime rub left over from the cheesemaking process, drizzle some onto the salad for extra kick and color.

BROWN BUTTER BURRATA

If you've ever had the (still somewhat rare) pleasure of tasting fresh burrata, you know that it is a delicate and tender pouch made of mozzarella-like cheese filled with a creamy ricotta-like curd. The result is a creation that tastes like it is made by unicorns on clouds. Unfortunately, it's not widely available in the United States, since it's hard to ship this highly perishable cheese from Italy (where the unicorns have their little outfit); one importer says you have maybe five days from the moment it's made. A perfect DIY cheese, right?

In adding brown butter to the filling, I made a bold move that, I dare say, raises this cheese to a different level. Give it a try and if it's too far past the classic for you, just replace the brown butter with plain heavy cream for the more traditional flavor.

Like many of the other cheeses in this section, shaping the burrata will take some practice. But even if your burrata pouches are messy piles of curd, proceed to drizzle them with the brown butter, and the flavor will carry you through mastery of the stuffing process. Just think, once you get it, the filling ideas are only limited by your imagination!

HOW EASY IS IT?

LEVEL: (Easy) Easier Easiest

READY TO EAT IN: 1 hour

MAKES: 1½ pounds

BIGGEST PAIN: Learning to fill and seal the pouches.

USES: Can be used like mozzarella, but is most often the main feature in an appetizer platter.

RECOMMENDED MILK: Whole cow's milk and cow's milk cream (also called heavy cream or whipping cream). The point here is creamy decadence, so use the real deal!

WORTH MENTIONING: This recipe relies on microwave use; alternate instructions for heating and stretching are included, but may take longer and give varied texture results.

INGREDIENTS

4 tablespoons salted butter

1½ teaspoons citric acid

½ cup plus ¼ cup dechlorinated water

¼ tablet vegetarian rennet

1 gallon whole cow's milk
(*not* ultra-pasteurized)

1 cup cream (*not* ultra-pasteurized),
optional

1¼ teaspoons flake salt, divided
into two ½ teaspoons and
one ¼ teaspoon

SUPPLIES

1 tablespoon

Saucepan

Large spoon

Small heat-proof bowl

1 teaspoon

½ teaspoon

½ cup

¼ cup

1 cup

5-quart stockpot

Large slotted spoon

Cooking thermometer

Large microwave-safe bowl

Small bowl

¼ teaspoon

Medium bowl

Plastic gloves, optional

Parchment or waxed paper, optional

PART 1: BROWNING THE BUTTER

1 Melt the 4 tablespoons of butter in a saucepan set over medium heat.

PART 2: MAKING THE CHEESE

1 Stir the citric acid into the ½ cup of water and set it aside.

YOU'RE MAKING BEURRE NOISETTE— IT'S A FRENCH THING!

2 Let it simmer and brown (don't walk away) for 4 to 6 minutes. Stir every minute or so to make sure the butter isn't burning. The color should turn dark amber, like weak coffee or strong tea.

MAKES EVERYTHING DELICIOUS!

3 Transfer the butter to a small heat-proof bowl and set it aside in a warm place. (Beautiful, isn't it?)

2 Dissolve the ¼ tablet of rennet in the ¼ cup of water and set it aside.

3 Pour the gallon of milk and the cup of cream into the pot.

4 Stir in the dissolved citric acid solution. Then heat the milk on medium to 90°F.

5 Add the rennet solution and mix it in with 20 quick strokes to make sure it is incorporated evenly.

8 Use the spoon to gently slice through any large clumps of curd so that the largest pieces are just 1 to 2 inches. Slowly move the pieces around in the pot for 1 to 2 minutes.

9 Avoid vigorously stirring the curds because this will break them into tiny pieces. Instead, slowly move the pieces around the pot to help them shrink, release more whey, and prepare the curds for the next heating and kneading steps.

6 You will see some separation between curds and whey, or the milk could look like shiny yogurt or clumps of cheese, and/or you could see a large curd mass that pulls away from the sides of the pot when you press it with the back of a spoon.

7 Without stirring, continue heating to 105°F (or 110°F if you will not be using a microwave for stretching the curd). You should see coagulation at 105°F but even if you don't, lower the heat and keep the curds at 105°F (or 110°F) for the following step.

10 You should see a change in the texture of the curds, from that of soft yogurt to that of scrambled eggs. If you do not, heat for an additional minute. Then turn off the heat and scoop the curds into the microwave-safe bowl.

11 Scoop 1 cup of the curds and place them in a small bowl. These will be used for the filling. Squeeze out any extra whey over the pot.

Yum, Yum, Yum, Yum, Yum. Yum!

12 To prepare the filling, gently mix the brown butter and ¼ teaspoon of the salt into the cup of curds in the bowl, breaking up the largest pieces as you stir.

13 The consistency of the filling is up to your personal taste, but traditionally it includes a balance of some curds, some liquid, and a not necessarily completely smooth texture. Set the filling aside in a warm place.

16 Heat the remaining portion of curds in the microwave for 25 seconds. Use the spoon or your hands to fold the curds over 4 to 5 times to evenly distribute the heat and to begin to gather the curds into a large mound.

17 Use the spoon to hold back the curds while you pour any released whey into the pot.

14 Divide the large bowl of curds (not buttered) into two equal portions.

15 Move one half (roughly 1 cup) into a medium bowl and set it aside.

18 Microwave the drained curds again for 25 seconds, add ½ teaspoon of the salt, fold the curds 15 times (or less, just until they hold together), and drain any excess whey.

19 You should start feeling a change in the texture of the curds: They may hold together better, feel more springy and stretchy, and may appear a little shinier.

20 Microwave again for 15 seconds. Fold the curds 5 times to distribute the heat and then knead the curds until you see a slight shine (the curd is quite hot now, so use a spoon or wear gloves if necessary).

21 The texture now resists in a clearly springy manner, and the curd easily forms a ball (it could take up to another 20 folds).

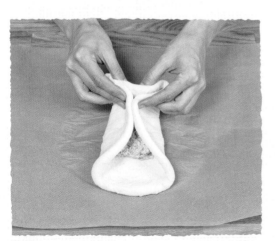

24 Bring four opposite edges of the flat circle to meet one another, keeping the creamy curds inside, and pinch the edges together to make a small pouch.

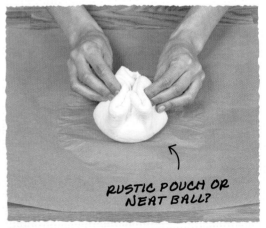

RUSTIC POUCH OR NEAT BALL?

25 Press the edges together to keep the pouch closed; the remaining heat will help seal them, as will the next step. You may serve the cheese as a rustic pouch, or . . .

22 Working quickly to retain heat, gather the ball of curd and flatten it into a circle on a sheet of parchment paper, leaving the middle slightly thicker than the edges. (If you need a little more heat to flatten the ball, microwave the curds for another 10 seconds.)

23 Scoop half of the reserved buttery curd filling from step 13 and pile it in the middle of the flattened circle of curd.

26 . . . wrap the paper around the pouch and twist the top tightly to make a ball. The cheese continues to melt, trapping the curds inside as it settles for just 5 to 10 minutes at room temperature.

27 Unwrap the cheese and flip it over to eat it at room temperature. The butter is oozy and the curd melts in your mouth. (Visually, it may flatten a little, but it's delicious and consistent with the traditionally loose look of these pouches.)

NOTE: Allow Brown Butter Burrata leftovers to come to room temperature or warm in the microwave for 10 to 20 seconds to soften the filling. (Cheesy tip: Did you know? Most cheeses are better eaten at room temperature!)

28 Repeat steps 14 to 27 with the second half of the curd. To serve, cut into the pouch to appreciate both layers of texture and flavor. Dip crispy slices of pear or apple right into the filling!

VARIATIONS + SUBSTITUTIONS

- Make old-school burrata with ¼ cup heavy cream in the filling instead of brown butter. If you make the filling with cream instead, you can cool the paper-wrapped pouch in the freezer for 5 minutes to retain the perky ball shape—the cream filling is not affected negatively by the cool temperature the way that the butter filling is.

- Fill the pouch with curds and anything you can imagine: ham, spinach, even a roasted fig! Who's to stop you (and who doesn't like to find a hidden surprise)?

- If you want to experiment, but want to start slowly, mix a little pesto in with the creamy filling (no brown butter needed).

SAUTÉED GRAPE AND PROSCIUTTO PLATTER

— SERVES 6 TO 8 —

Burrata is already fit for a special occasion simply because of its rich flavor. This presentation will elevate it to holiday or special dinner party status. It's rich enough that folks will just take a bite or two, so it goes a long way.

2 tablespoons butter (page 236)

1 cup green or red grapes, whole or sliced in half

8 slices prosciutto

1 pouch of Brown Butter Burrata

Coarsely cracked black peppercorns

Melt the butter in a hot cast-iron skillet, over medium heat. Sauté the grapes just until they soften a little and glisten, about 3 minutes. Meanwhile, arrange the prosciutto slices around the edge of a plate and place the entire pouch of burrata in the middle with the seam facedown (smooth dome on top). Trim (and eat) the seals if necessary.

Top the burrata with the warm grapes (and of course the extra butter). Sprinkle the platter with cracked peppercorns. Dig, family-style, into this luscious appetizer!

It's rich, so you'll want to share, and follow it up with something green and crisp. For variety, you can easily replace the grapes with fresh figs, apricots, or plums.

Chapter 3

SHAPES AND FLAVORS

PRESENTATION:
Hand-Shaping and DIY Molds

Perhaps the most exciting part about making your own cheese in one hour (aside from eating it, of course) is being able to customize it to your specifications. Don't know where to start? Browse your cupboards for interesting containers for the shaping recommendations. Then turn to the fancy cheese aisle at your local grocery store for flavor ideas or try starting with a theme—foods eaten in autumn, for example, like cranberry sauce, pumpkin pie . . . or what about mixing dried cranberries and fresh nutmeg into Fromage Facile (page 43) for a nice bagel spread? Great for a fall brunch! I'm often inspired by a specific person and his or her favorite treats, by holidays, seasonal produce, desserts, savory snacks, international cuisine, other cheeses, or even colors. It's a fun game once you get going, and the combinations are as endless as they are surprising.

Shaping Firm Curd

If you don't intend to cook with your firm cheeses right away, shaping cheeses like Chivo Fresco (page 75), Curried Paneer (page 67), and Smoky Cheater (page 103) makes for nifty presentation and a whole lot of fun for you! Some of these techniques will not take any longer than the suggested shaping method given in the recipe; others, I have to admit, really indulge in the geeky craft of it! Save those for times when you can plan ahead and/or when the party is about making the cheese rather than eating it . . . primarily anyway.

You don't have to go out and buy professional molds and presses for our one-hour cheeses. Look around your kitchen and see if you can imagine cheese in the shape of cookie cutters, measuring cups, tart pans, sushi rice molds, and even edible molds like red bell peppers!

MOLDING

If you've tried your hand at making the Triple Pepper Hack (page 129) or Smoky Cheater (page 103), you're already an expert on simple molding of cheese for presentation. But let's review:

SUPPLIES

- Measuring cup or other firm container
- Cheesecloth, plastic cling wrap, or parchment paper, optional
- Firm cheese curds

1 Spoon the warm, salted curds into your mold of choice—a measuring cup, bowl, tart pan, and so on. Optional: Line the bowl with cheesecloth, plastic cling wrap, or parchment paper for different surface textures as well as for fail-safe unmolding. Cover loosely with more parchment paper or waxed paper.

RED BELL PEPPER   COOKIE CUTTER

MEASURING CUP   PLASTIC MOLD   TART PAN

2 Press the curds firmly into the mold, then chill it in the freezer for 10 to 15 minutes—this will help the cheese hold its shape.

3 Invert the measuring cup or bowl with a hard knock onto a flat surface to release your wheel, or pull it up by the liner (if you used one).

VOILÁ! A MEASURING CUP CREATES A SMALL WHEEL OF CHEESE!

VARIATIONS + SUBSTITUTIONS

• Try other edible molds (besides the red bell pepper shown). Use a knife to trim or hollow out vegetables and fruits like cucumbers, colorful heirloom tomatoes, apples, pears, figs, and plums. They are best when sliced into cross sections for a delicious and beautiful combination of flavors, colors, and textures. And in case it's not obvious, do not unmold them!

• Use any food-safe container for a variety of shapes and sizes. Cupcake pans make nice medallions, measuring spoons are great for bites, and bowls make excellent wheels.

CUTTING

The traditional cheese wheel is a lovely way to present your homemade cheese, but don't feel that you have to be limited by round or rectangular containers. You can branch out—way out! If opening your lunch box at work to see a star- or heart-shaped cheese snack looking back at you makes you giddy, here is an opportunity to get even more crafty. There are as many options for cutting cheese (not to be confused with "cutting the cheese") as there are for molding cheese. Use cookie cutters, a knife, biscuit cutters, or a cup to carve out shapes from firm cheese. Create an entire batch and choose a theme or make all different shapes. This is also a good use of leftover cheese (just slice a piece that is 2 inches thick and at least as big as the cookie cutter you plan to use).

SUPPLIES

- **Flat glass dish**
- **Parchment or wax paper**
- **Firm cheese curds**
- **Cookie cutters, biscuit cutter, cup, or knife**

1 Line the flat dish with parchment or wax paper. Press fresh, warm, and salted curd onto it until it is at least 1 inch deep, making sure that the top is even. Cover it and allow it to cool and firm in the fridge for at least 2 hours.

4 If needed, gently push the cheese out with your fingers. If it sticks, try dipping your cookie cutters into water or olive oil.

2 Release the firm curd onto a flat surface like a counter or cutting board. Plan the placement of your cutters on the curd before cutting.

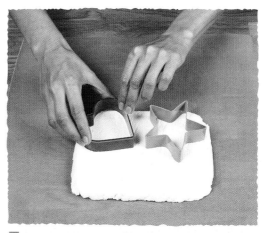

3 Press the cutters into the curd and wiggle them just a little to make sure you cut all the way through the curd.

5 It's easy to get clear shapes with simple cookie cutters (cutters with really detailed nooks and crannies don't work as well). Cut up any leftover bits and create an Olive Oil and Herbs jar, page 204.

VARIATIONS + SUBSTITUTIONS

As in decorating cookies, cutting your shapes is only the beginning! You can go from there and embellish, using herbs, spices, edible flowers, dried fruit, and even fresh veggies or pickles. (See how the bunny's peppercorn eyes and rosemary whiskers make it come *alive*?!) Cover a heart with crushed pink peppercorns, dot the points of a star with pointy herb leaves—tap into your inner preschooler (better yet, have one help you)! See the Flavoring section, page 206, for more on using edibles to flavor and decorate your shaped cheeses.

Shaping Soft Curd

Soft curd can be shaped much like firm curd, but because of its relatively fragile nature, it requires a more delicate touch. Pressing, for instance, is not generally required beyond making sure you've gotten rid of any big gaps and air bubbles in the curd.

When scouting for molds in your kitchen, consider containers that require less handling than the ones you used for firm curd. Scoopers, measuring spoons, paper cupcake liners, parchment paper, and sushi mats all fit the bill, but experiment!

The curd is easier to shape when cool, so chill it in the freezer for 10 to 15 minutes or let it sit in the fridge for a couple of hours after draining for best results. Take it out, and stir and knead it gently with a spoon to create a very smooth consistency before shaping.

SUSHI MAT · WAX PAPER · ICE CREAM SCOOP

MEASURING SPOON · MUFFIN TIN · CUPCAKE LINERS · PARCHMENT PAPER

THE CLASSIC PARTY LOG

You can use plain parchment paper or even your bare hands to make a rustic cheese log, but a sushi mat helps create a consistent roll—and a cool bamboo imprint! It's a very inexpensive investment if you don't already have one, and it makes rolling a cinch.

SUPPLIES

- Parchment or waxed paper
- Bamboo sushi mat
- Spoon
- Soft cheese curds

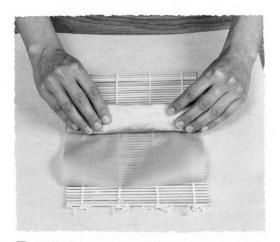

3 Roll the curd tightly in the paper first.

1 Line the sushi mat with parchment or waxed paper.

2 Spoon the curd evenly across one short side about 2 inches from the edge.

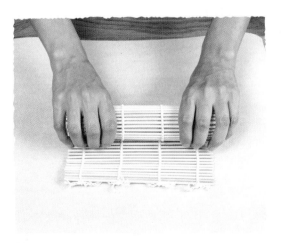

4 Then roll the mat very tightly around the paper log. Squeeze and roll the mat, applying even pressure to make sure the log is even.

5 Open up the mat and paper. Smooth any gaps and even out the ends if they don't match each other. The cheese log is ready to roll in spices, minced herbs, crushed nuts, diced dried fruit, or even flower petals (see page 206)!

PETITE BONBONS

Roll these little cheese morsels in a variety of
flavorful and colorful edibles to really delight your
party table. Soft shaping can be done by hand just
like Chèvre French Kisses (page 49, for a casual
look) or by scooping rounded little bonbons to be
displayed on mini cupcake liners (for a fancy look).

SUPPLIES

- Mini cupcake liners or candy cups
- Cookie dough scoop (or melon baller) or
  measuring spoon
- Soft cheese curds

1 Using a cookie dough scoop or measuring
spoon to shape the bonbons, carve out a small bit
of curd from the bowl.

2 Press the soft curd into the scoop just enough
to rid it of air bubbles.

3 Drop the bonbon into a mini cupcake liner.
Repeat as many times as needed to use the rest of
the curd. The bonbons are ready to eat—or ready
to take on any toppings!

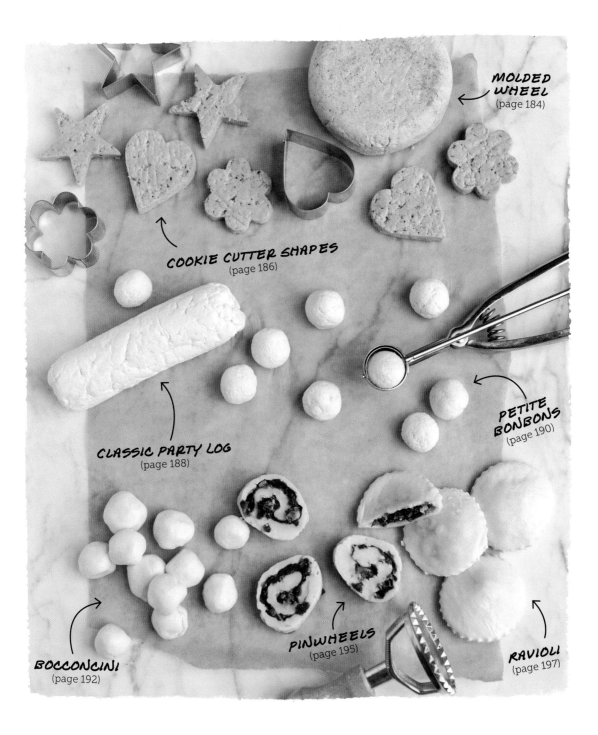

MOLDED
WHEEL
(page 184)

COOKIE CUTTER SHAPES
(page 186)

CLASSIC PARTY LOG
(page 188)

PETITE
BONBONS
(page 190)

BOCCONCINI
(page 192)

PINWHEELS
(page 195)

RAVIOLI
(page 197)

Shaping Pulled Curd

You've already seen several ways to shape pulled curd cheeses—from the Brown Butter Burrata (page 171) to the Chipotle-Lime Oaxaca (page 161) to the Favorite Melty Mozzarella (page 137)—so you have the basic techniques. Here's to going a little further!

BOCCONCINI

Sure, you can cut cubes of mozzarella and toss them in vinaigrette for a delicious marinated appetizer, but this method is worth it if you want to make legit-looking, marinated bocconcini (Italian for "little mouthfuls") for a party, or to give as a gift. Finish the look by marinating in a pretty jar (page 204). Feel free to start with plain or flavored curd, since it does not matter for this process.

SUPPLIES

- Pulled cheese curd from Favorite Melty Mozzarella
- Parchment or waxed paper (slightly wider than the length of the pulled curd)
- Cotton twine (twice as long as the pulled curd)

1 Prepare a pulled rope of Favorite Melty Mozzarella, much like you do to make Pizza Filata. See pages 137–149.

LEAVE A SHORT TAIL

4 Wrap the long end of twine around the roll, about 1½ inches from the end.

2 Center the rope horizontally across the parchment (about 2–3 inches on each side, and roll the mozzarella tightly. Twist and pinch the ends closed.

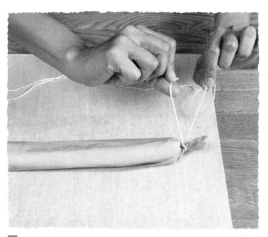

3 Tie one end of the roll with one end of twine, keeping a long length of twine to work with.

HOLD THE SHORT TAIL AS YOU WORK.

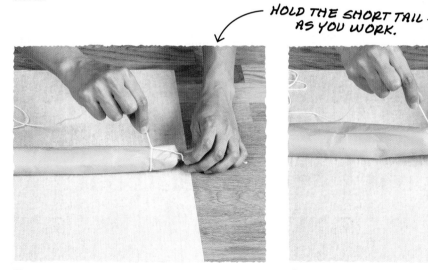

5 Thread the twine end under the loop you just made to complete a simple knot.

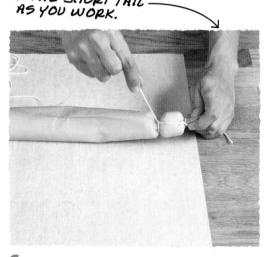

6 Pull tightly on both ends of the knot, nearly pinching off your first little bite. Repeat the loop-and-knot sequence, about 1½ inches from the previous loop and knot.

7 Continue the knotting, trying your best to maintain even spacing that will result in consistent size bites.

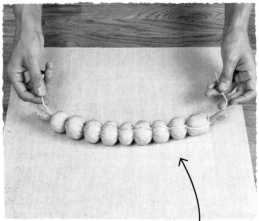

8 Tie and tighten the last knot and briefly admire your handiwork before disassembly.

IT WILL LOOK A LITTLE LIKE A WEIRD, BEADED CHEESE NECKLACE.

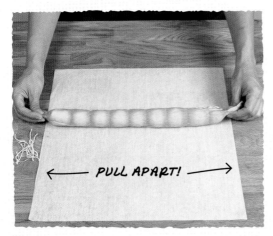

← *PULL APART!* →

9 Snip off the twine and pull the ends of the parchment in opposite directions.

10 Unroll the parchment, and the resulting bocconcini is ready to toss in vinaigrette, herbs, garlic, and so on, or serve as is. (Note: For a cool party trick, tie up the rope in advance but wait to unwrap the bites in front of your guests.)

PINWHEELS

Gluten-free folks will rejoice when they see these flatbread-free appetizers, but these can also make a nice Caprese side salad for anyone or, depending on the stuffing, a main course! Try prosciutto, grilled zucchini, olive tapenade . . . the possibilities are limitless.

SUPPLIES

- Oval sheet of mozzarella (or other pulled curd cheese, flattened per the instructions for Brown Butter Burrata, page 171)
- Parchment or waxed paper (slightly larger than the sheet of mozzarella)
- Fillings: basil leaves, sun-dried tomatoes, arugula leaves (or anything else you enjoy)

1 Lay the flattened oval onto a sheet of parchment paper, and gather your fillings. (Note: Oily or wet fillings may make it difficult for your pinwheel to seal.) The size of the oval is flexible.

2 Place the fillings flat onto the sheet of cheese, covering the surface except for the edges, which should be left plain in order to seal the pinwheels.

3 Starting at one long edge, roll up the cheese lengthwise, trapping the toppings inside. Use the edge of the paper to help start the roll if necessary.

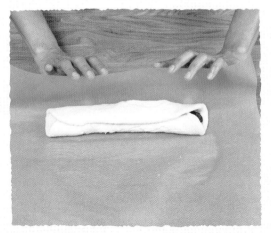

4 Continue to roll the cheese, tucking in any toppings that escape out the sides. Then roll the parchment around the mozzarella roll.

5 Squeeze firmly as you roll—enough to make sure the contents are snuggly wrapped but not so much that the roll becomes uneven.

6 Unwrap the parchment from the roll and slice the cheese into 1- to 2-inch pinwheels (depending on your appetite!).

7 Plate and serve the pinwheels.

ENJOY!

RAVIOLI

Who doesn't love ravioli? Those squishy clouds filled with more creamy deliciousness . . . I can't even think of a way that they could be made any better. Oh, wait, I can: Why not replace the pasta dough with cheese? Fill these with your favorite veggies or meats, pour warm sauce right over them, and enjoy—and then apply the same technique to any dumpling-like delicacy: gyoza, egg rolls, empanadas, pierogi, and so on.

SUPPLIES

- 2 sheets of mozzarella (Favorite Melty Mozzarella, page 137)
  Note: 8 inches × 6 inches is a good size for two people
- Parchment paper
- Knife, ravioli cutter, or pizza cutter
- Teaspoon
- About 1 cup of filling of choice (sautéed spinach and mushrooms, sun-dried tomatoes and shredded basil, leftover ham frittata, grilled peppers and onions, olive tapenade, sausage and olives)
- Fork

1 Flatten the two sheets of mozzarella to about ¼-inch thickness on parchment paper. Score each sheet into sixths—but don't cut all the way through. (Note: If you are lucky enough to have a ravioli pan, lay one sheet on the pan.)

2 Place a teaspoonful (less if you're making tiny ravioli, more if you're going for a meal-size hand pie!) of your filling onto each ravioli section on one ravioli sheet.

3 Carefully cover the filled sheet of cheese with the plain sheet.

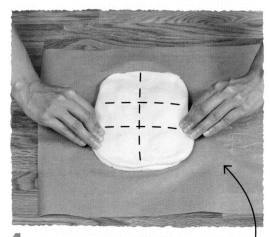

4 Gently press the top sheet around the edges and between the filling "pockets."

PRESS BETWEEN THE POCKETS, TOO.

5 Trim the edges, and slice through the pressed sections to make separate ravioli (use a knife, pizza cutter, or scalloped ravioli cutter), and press fork tines around the edges to seal them if necessary.

6 Eat as hand pies, or enjoy with marinara sauce or pesto just as you would traditional ravioli. Remember: This is not actually pasta, but deliciously melty cheese, so keep the sauce warm but not piping hot!

Wrapping Cheese

Cheesemakers around the world are creative people, wrapping up their French goat cheeses in spirit-soaked grape leaves for some added flavor and covering their juicy burrata in palm leaves for storage and presentation. These are just two of the nifty wrappings you can use—but break out the chard leaves, nori (seaweed), corn husks, and preserved grape leaves (they don't need to be soaked in spirits) for a few more options. Need I tell you by now that this is very easy to do yourself? Let's use grape leaves as an example.

SUPPLIES

- Parchment paper or a clean flat surface
- 3 preserved grape leaves ← *LOOK FOR THEM AT A MEDITERRANEAN GROCERY.*
- A small wheel or wedge of cheese
- Fresh sage leaf or other herb, optional

1 Arrange 3 large grape leaves on the parchment paper to create a solid foundation—no holes.

2 Place your cheese in the center (I added a sage leaf for interest and flavor) and start folding the leaves into the center and over the cheese.

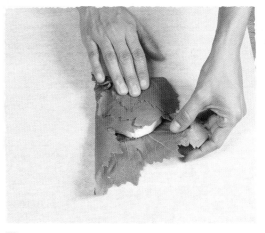

3 Continue folding up all of the leaves until you have a tidy packet.

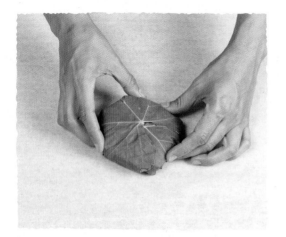

NOTE: To store, refrigerate in a covered container for 1 day (or more, if you don't mind a green tint and a tangy flavor infusion).

4 Flip the packet over so the leaves' veins are visible. You're done! Eat fresh, or brush the packet with olive oil and grill just a bit until browned. Unwrap the packet to eat (or cut right into it since the grape leaves are delicious).

VARIATIONS + SUBSTITUTIONS

• Decorate your cool little cheese packets with scallion ties, herbs, edible flowers, and peppers. Use hidden toothpicks to hold the packets closed if necessary, but remember to remove them before eating!

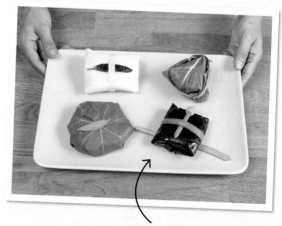

TRY WARMING THESE ON A GRILL!

HERB-INFUSED OLIVE OIL
AND CHEESE
(page 204)

Thank You!

LEAF-WRAPPED CHEESE
(page 199)

EDIBLE
FLOWERS
(page 206)

DRY HERBS
AND SPICES
(page 208)

LAYERED
FLAVOR
(page 210)

CUSTOM FLAVOR:
Herbs, Spices, and Edible Flowers

Savory additions to your cheeses, like herbs, spices, and even edible flowers, are about dressing up your cheese in style while adding to its flavor. (After all, your cheese is not just a pretty face—there's real character underneath!) Here are a few suggestions for getting to know your herb garden (or your flower garden) and applying your harvest to your cheese presentation.

Olive Oil and Herbs

Any cheese that will retain its shape after it's cut can be put in a clear jar, topped with extra-virgin olive oil, and infused with garlic and herbs. It makes a nice last-minute appetizer, or can be made, assembly-line-style, for everyone on your gift list. An added bonus: It helps preserve your one-hour cheese for about another five days in the fridge and is a great use for leftover bits of cheese (if there is such a thing!) Vary the herbs with the seasons for a variety of flavors and colors.

NOTE: Pizza Filata (page 151), Chivo Fresco (page 75), and Triple Pepper Hack (used here, page 129), all make great choices, but all cheeses that keep their shape when cut will work nicely.

SUPPLIES

- ½ cup of firm cheese (for one jar)
- Knife
- 2 sprigs or 5 leaves of fresh herbs (or ½ teaspoon of dried herbs)
- 1 to 2 garlic cloves, to taste
- 10 rainbow peppercorns
- Clear 8-ounce jar with tight-fitting lid
- Pinch of sea salt
- ½ cup extra-virgin olive oil

1 Gather the ingredients and cut the firm cheese into ½- to 1-inch cubes.

4 All the contents should be submerged in oil.

2 Add alternating layers of cheese cubes and add-ins (herbs, garlic, peppercorns) to the jar. Top everything with a pinch or two of salt.

3 Carefully pour the olive oil into the jar.

5 Top the jar with its lid and store it in the refrigerator for a minimum of 4 hours to allow the flavors to develop. The flavors will get more pronounced the longer the cheese is allowed to infuse with the herbs and garlic.

NOTE: Keeping the cheese in oil and away from air preserves it longer. The olive oil will get cloudy when chilled in the fridge but it will clear up after 15 minutes or so on your counter.

Edible Flowers
and Whole Herbs

Beyond that herb garden you may have growing in a pot in your kitchen, edible flowers are all around us, too.

Lavender, sage, thyme, chives, sweet pea, arugula flowers, and mini roses (in multiple colors!), are all fairly easy to come by. If you don't have a garden, scout out the neighborhood—if you find some good specimens, just ask. Who wouldn't trade edible flowers and herbs for some fresh cheese? (Just ask your neighbors if they spray their garden with insecticides or anything else you do not wish to ingest before you pick. You may also want to aim high to avoid dog-level, if you know what I mean.) While you're at it, gather whole herbs like sage leaves, rosemary, basil, mint, arugula leaves, pea shoots, dill leaves, fennel, and asparagus fronds.

These lovely splashes of color and flavor will open up a whole new world of cheese decor for you. It's terribly romantic and even breathtaking at times.

SUPPLIES

- **Variety of fresh edible flowers and herbs**
- **Parchment paper or a clean flat surface**
- **1 small cheese wheel, firm or soft**

1 Like an artist at the palette, collect and select an array of fresh edible flowers and whole herbs, like rose petals, asparagus fronds, and tiny bergamot mint leaves (shown).

4 Just use the moisture of the cheese as glue! Top the wheel with a complementary add-on like a sprinkling of cracked pepper and honey or cracked pistachios and ground cardamom. I used an asparagus frond and tiny mint leaves.

2 Taste a nibble to familiarize yourself with any new flavors and textures. You want them to complement the cheese you have chosen, so taste a little bit of your cheese with tiny bits of your flowers and herbs.

3 With the round of cheese centered on the parchment paper, apply each flower or herb by pressing it gently into the side of the cheese.

NOTE: A very hot wheel will wilt tender flowers and herbs, but temperature does not matter otherwise.

5 Serve it alongside other decorative wheels, and you'll have a mini garden on your cheese plate—ready for a tea party! Keep it simple, like the thyme flower–piled chèvre (top), or re-create the pea shoot and flower mozzarella (left).

VARIATIONS + SUBSTITUTIONS

- For large edible flowers like zucchini, try stuffing the blossom with cheese. The blossoms are great when dipped in batter and fried, but even when wrapped simply around the wheel, like grape leaves (pages 199–200), they are lovely.

Dry Herbs and Spices

Thankfully, there is more than one way your cheese can win points for presentation. If whole herbs and edible flowers aren't your thing, turn to your spice rack for the dry stuff. Whether you are coating your cheeses (this page) or layering your cheeses with spices (page 210), cracked black pepper, oregano, basil, lavender, caraway seeds, and specialty salts are all easy embellishments to dress your soft cheese in.

COATING IN TASTY BITS

All manner of tasty bits can enhance your cheese. Cover rolls, wheels, and your custom shapes in any of the herbs, seeds, or salts mentioned above, but don't stop there. Aromatic spices such as smoked paprika and cinnamon or crushed nuts like toasted pine nuts or pecans lend vibrant colors, textures, and flavors that really add drama to any homemade cheese plate.

SUPPLIES

- Parchment paper
- Log or miniwheel of soft, cooled cheese curds (see Classic Party Log, page 188, still in its paper wrapper, or Petite Bonbons, page 190)
- Dried herbs (oregano, basil, lavender, etc.)

PARCHMENT PAPER = EASY CLEANUP!

1 Lay down a sheet of parchment paper on your work surface for easy cleanup. Spread a generous amount of the dried herbs across the parchment.

4 You may have to sprinkle extra herbs on the ends and pat them in place.

2 Gently unroll the paper and place the soft cheese on the herbs.

3 Roll the cheese back and forth in the herbs to coat the surface.

PARTY LOG!

5 Once you're content with the amount of herb coverage on the log, it's ready to party (aka serve and slice).

VARIATIONS + SUBSTITUTIONS

- Start with a variety of shaped soft curd as your blank canvas.

- Rather than coat the entire log or miniwheel, cover parts selectively.

LAYERING FLAVOR

There's something alluring about that line of blue mold in blue cheese or vegetable ash in French cheeses. That line is very easy to create, One-Hour Cheese–style, with fine herbs or spices.

SUPPLIES

- Spoon
- Soft cheese curds
- Cheese mold

    Note: I used traditional, semi-translucent cheese molds here so you can see the layers, but cups or bowls work just as well.

- Selection of dried herbs (I used dill)

1 Scoop half of the curds you intend to use into the mold to form the first layer; it will be the top layer when you invert the wheel.

LIKE FLOURING A CAKE PAN!

CLOSE-UP
Wipe the inside of the mold with your index finger so that the second layer is not freckled with herbs.

4 Pat the side of the mold as you turn it, shifting the herbs so they sprinkle to cover the first layer. Knock out any excess herbs.

5 Cover the thin herb layer with the remaining curd—if you halved it, the second layer should be of approximately equal thickness to the first—and press it firmly into the mold.

2 Use the spoon to smooth the layer, keeping in mind that the line of herbs will rest on the surface you create.

3 Sprinkle a thin layer of herbs on the flattened curd. The layer should be visible, but not so thick that it will prevent the second layer from sticking.

6 Smooth out the surface, turn over the mold, and deliver a good whack to the bottom so the cheese wheel drops onto your platter.

VARIATIONS + SUBSTITUTIONS

- The layering technique also works well with diced dried fruit like golden apricots, diced olives, or ground sumac, shown here in the smaller wheel.

Chapter 4

THE DIY CHEESE PLATTER

PAIRINGS AND ACCOMPANIMENTS

Even though cheese by itself is a near-perfect snack, here's the deal with accompaniments, and why they're worth the DIY effort: They can complement the cheeses on your platter with crisp or chewy textures, juiciness, freshness, salty dryness, and various other delights. The contrasts and variety make the experience more than a snack but rather a culinary experience. In addition, a well-balanced platter gives you the opportunity to cleanse your palate between cheeses—which allows you to have that "first-bite taste" more than once! Assuming you've already made the cheese, you're probably ready to get out of the kitchen and eat, so all these delicious accompaniments are ready to serve in short amounts of time. Simple goodness—are you in?

DOCTOR IT UP: Simple Ways to Customize Store-Bought Goodies

In less than ten minutes, you can turn store-bought pantry and fridge basics into impressive fancy foods that act as the entourage and supporting cast to your homemade cheese—perfect for those impromptu hangouts and last-minute dinner parties!

Fancy Nuts

Fancy nuts can be made with any combination of nuts or seeds and any herbs, spices, salts, and even oil or honey that complement your cheeses. Use the ratios in the recipe as starting points, but adjust as your taste buds tell you or if you're using something very strong like cayenne or honey. These Sea Salt and Rosemary Almonds are great with pretty much any cheese (or, dare I say, on their own!), but I especially like the crunchy salty contrast with mild and creamy cheeses like Fromage Facile (page 43).

> *TIP!* Nuts are best kept in the freezer because their oils can become rancid. That way, you'll always have a stash at the ready (and not waste your money).

SEA SALT AND ROSEMARY ALMONDS
SERVES: 4 TO 6

INGREDIENTS

- **2 cups roasted almonds (salted is okay)**
  Note: If you can find Spanish Marcona almonds, they are a special treat!
- **1 to 2 teaspoons extra-virgin olive oil**
- **2 teaspoons fresh rosemary, finely minced**
- **Flaky sea salt to taste**

1. Pour the almonds and 1 teaspoon of olive oil into a deep bowl and toss until the almonds are covered.

2. If you see some dry almonds, add a little more olive oil, a quarter teaspoon at a time (they should not be dripping—just enough to allow the herbs to stick).

3. Add the rosemary and salt and mix thoroughly. All done, and they're ready to serve.

Optional: If you have an extra 5 minutes, serve the nuts warm! Preheat the oven to 350°F, then bake them on a cookie sheet, watching for browning (you want them just warm and fragrant), about 5 minutes. (Note: Different nuts and seeds will toast faster than others, so be vigilant! Pumpkin seeds pop when they're toasting, so don't be alarmed, just make sure to take them out before they burn.)

- hazelnuts, cacao powder, chili powder, sea salt, hazelnut oil

- pecans, cracked black pepper, sea salt, honey (instead of oil)

- walnuts, cinnamon, cayenne, sea salt, ghee

- pumpkin seeds, curry powder, lemon zest, sea salt, olive oil

5-MINUTE CHEESE PLATTER

Invited your coworkers over after work for a cheese-tasting? Just execute a minor fridge and pantry raid for nuts, olives, or pickles; dried fruit like dates, figs, and prunes; honey (with honeycomb is even better!) and marmalades; and fresh fruit like grapes, berries, or apple slices. They're all great accompaniments to cheese. Make neat little piles of the scavenged items on a large platter and just add cheese(s)! It's quick, it's easy, and it should be enough to tide over a small group.

JUST WAITING FOR THE DOCTOR!

MEDITERRANEAN
OLIVES
(page 217)

GRILLED
HALOUMI
(page 93)

JICAMA
CRISPS
(page 218)

SEA SALT AND
ROSEMARY
ALMONDS
(page 214)

WALNUT-FILLED
DATES
(page 217)

Fruit and Nut Bites

The original reason fruit was dried was so that it could be preserved beyond its season. Today that shelf life means it's a flexible last-minute party food! You can stock your pantry with a variety of dried fruit for any cheesy occasion. Try these sweet and savory dates with the Brown Butter Burrata (page 171) or Chèvre French Kisses (page 49).

WALNUT-FILLED DATES

SERVES: 4 TO 6

INGREDIENTS

- 8 medjool dates
- Flaky sea salt (if the walnuts are unsalted)
- 16 large walnut pieces

1. Cut or tear each date in half and remove the pit as well as any little stem that remains at one end.

2. Line up the date halves split-side up, and lightly sprinkle them with the sea salt.

3. Press a walnut piece into the cavity of each date half—in place of the pit—until it's snug. Done!

OTHER SUGGESTED COMBINATIONS

- Dried golden apricots halves, roasted/salted cashews, cracked pepper

- Dried mission fig halves, roasted/salted almonds, minced thyme

- Do you have a few more minutes? Wrap the nutty fruit in bacon and secure using a toothpick. Bake the bundles at 350°F until the bacon is crispy, about 15 minutes!

MEDITERRANEAN OLIVES

SERVES: 4

Always keep a large jar or two of olives in your fridge: They won't go bad, and they're the perfect accompaniment to the firmer cheeses on your list. Bring them out just before party time and mix in some tasty bits to create your own olive bar. My local Lebanese grocer has an amazing variety of olives in cans, jars, or even bags, but any grocery store will carry something you can use. Mediterranean olives pair especially well with Chivo Fresco (page 75), Favorite Melty Mozzarella (page 137), and plain paneer (see variation, page 72).

INGREDIENTS

- 1 cup plain Kalamata olives
- 1 teaspoon chili pepper flakes
- 2 teaspoons za'atar, dried thyme, or oregano
- Squeeze of lemon juice
- Drizzle of extra-virgin olive oil

TIP! Try za'atar, a Mediterranean tangy herb mix made of thyme, sumac, and sesame seeds often eaten with olive oil and flat bread. If not, substitute with dried thyme or oregano.

1. Combine everything in a mixing bowl and toss until the olives are completely coated.

2. Serve immediately, or let the olives marinate in the fridge until party time.

OTHER SUGGESTED COMBINATIONS

- Spanish green olives, oregano, sun-dried tomatoes in oil, black pepper

- Oil-cured black olives (not the common black pizza olives), fresh minced parsley, lime zest, squeeze of lime juice

Raw Crisps

Some cheeses are even better with a fresh, juicy, and sometimes even sweet sidekick. Fruits and veggies might initially seem *meh* when you're talking about something as fancy as homemade one-hour cheese, but when sliced thinly and paired well, they can really be something special and provide that palate cleanser between more flavorful bites. Depending on the texture, you can use a slice of veggie to scoop cheese or just crunch on the side—just as you would crackers on a fancy cheese platter. Check out the recommendations below, or seek out whatever's in season for the best flavor and crunch. Raw crisps are great with every single cheese in this book but especially the rich and creamy Brown Butter Burrata (page 171) and Meyer Lemon Ricotta (page 35).

JICAMA CRISPS
SERVES: 4 TO 6

Jicama's simple flavor and fresh crunch is perfect with flavorful cheeses like the Triple Pepper Hack (page 129) or Smoky Cheater (page 103). For best results, slice the crisps right before you intend to eat them.

INGREDIENTS

- **Jicama or Japanese/seedless cucumber**

1. Peel the jicama.
2. Use a sharp knife or mandoline slicer to cut extra thin slices (half moons or wide strips).

OTHER SUGGESTED COMBINATIONS

- Bosc pears: Make a stack with slices of Farm-Fresh Rounds (page 123) or Favorite Melty Mozzarella (page 137).

- Rainbow radishes: Top with a schmear of Fromage Facile (page 43) and minced chives.

- Cucumber, beet, or kohlrabi pickles: Slice them thinly or just serve whole with grilled Haloumi? Halou-You! (page 93) or panfried Curried Paneer cubes (page 67).

- Dehydrated, crisp cross-sectional slices of sweet potato, tomatoes, apples, or blood oranges: Use as crackers and top with soft cheeses.

BUTTERNUT AND CHIVE CROSTINI
(page 221)

CHÈVRE FRENCH KISSES
(page 49)

SALAMI CRACKERS
(page 222)

PLANTAIN AND CRACKED PEPPER CRACKERS
(page 220)

GARLIC AND RAINBOW PEPPER OLIVE OIL CRISPBREAD
(page 222)

WHIP IT UP: 15-Minute Recipes and Formulas for Custom Pairings

Fruity pastes, dainty crostini, glossy fruit compotes, and crisp olive oil crackers are ever enticing at the cheese counters, but they can also be quite expensive. The ingredients used to make them, however, are generally pretty simple. With these tips, and about 15 minutes (or less!) on the clock, you can easily re-create your own delicious cheese party sides—so go ahead, dazzle your guests.

Crackers, Crostini, and Other Crunchy Pleasures

It's simple enough to find crackers in a vast array of flavors, shapes, and textures: There are really grainy, seed-filled crackers, or plain soda crackers meant to simply cleanse your palate or add a nice crunch; there are gluten-free and rice-based options; and I even saw crisp dehydrated blood orange and green apple slices at my cheese counter recently (and ran home to hook up my dehydrator). These are all delicious. Knock yourself out at the cracker aisle *but*, if you're craving something different or are really going for a theme that a wheat cracker just doesn't fit into, try baking or frying thin slices of these. . . .

TIP! Not all plantains are created equal! If you use a ripe yellow and brown plantain rather than a green one, you will end up with a sweet caramelized and soft treat. Still yummy (and great with ricotta!) but more of a condiment than a cracker—just go with it, but keep an eye out for green plantains for these crisp crackers.

PLANTAIN AND CRACKED PEPPER CRACKERS

SERVES: 4

These are my favorite homemade crackers. That's all. I just really, really think you should try them. If you've ever had Puerto Rican tostones, this flavor will be very familiar to you.

INGREDIENTS

- 1 large green plantain
- 4 tablespoons coconut oil or ghee (see page 240), for frying
- Sea salt and coarse cracked black pepper to taste

1. Peel the plantain (you may need a knife) and slice into very thin rounds, mimicking the thickness of a cracker.

2. Heat just enough coconut oil or ghee to coat a hot cast-iron skillet over medium-high heat, adding more oil as it is absorbed.

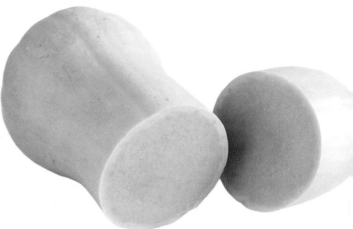

3. Fry the plantain crackers on both sides, until crispy and golden (do not allow them to overlap), about 2 minutes per side.

4. Remove the crackers and blot on paper towels. Sprinkle with sea salt and coarse cracked pepper. Your crackers are ready to dip or eat alongside your cheeses!

BUTTERNUT AND CHIVE CROSTINI

SERVES: 4

Crostini don't have to be made of baguette—try squash or root veggies for fun variety and color. Butternut squash is my favorite because of its long, seedless neck and tendency to caramelize around the edges. Thin slices crisp up nicely!

INGREDIENTS

- Butternut squash
- 2 tablespoons coconut oil, melted
- Sea salt to taste
- 2-4 teaspoons chives, finely minced

1. Preheat the oven to 375°F.

2. Cut the squash in half, widthwise. Set aside the fatter half that contains the seeds. (You can make oven fries with that end later using the same technique!) Peel the seedless piece of squash with a vegetable peeler, then cut off and discard the stem. Slice the remaining cylinder into very thin disks (a mandoline slicer is ideal for this but a sharp knife will work, too).

3. Toss the squash slices in a bowl with the coconut oil, salt, and chives. It's important that every piece be coated in oil, so use more if your squash is larger than average.

4. Place the coated squash slices on a cookie sheet in a single layer and bake for 20 minutes, flipping after 10 minutes, and checking frequently, since their thickness may vary depending on your slicing tool. The crostini are ready when they are crispy (not "raw crunchy") and browned in some spots. Sprinkle with fresh chives.

5. Allow the crostini to cool, sprinkle with more fresh chives if desired, and start stacking with Meyer Lemon Ricotta (page 35), Chèvre French Kisses (page 49), or any other cheese you fancy.

OTHER SUGGESTED COMBINATIONS

Try these frying and baking methods with thinly sliced acorn squash, sweet potatoes, turnips, beets, daikon radish, carrots, leek strips, and large sage leaves—they all make great crackers! Remember, you don't always need to be able to scoop cheese with your crackers. You just need a pleasing crunch to accompany your cheese. For example, sage leaves and leeks won't be able to hold cheese, but you will surely enjoy their smoky crispness alongside Triple Pepper Hack (page 129).

SALAMI CRACKERS

SERVES: 4

I discovered this cracker one morning when
I craved bacon but didn't have it. So I fried up
some salami instead, and a star was born! So easy
and so delicious. I began scheming other uses
immediately (see Salami Pockets, page 159). I
recommend any presliced variety because the thin,
uniform slices make the crispiest crackers. I use an
uncured variety but both cured and uncured salami
work—the little bowl shapes made by the slices are
ideal for cradling cheese.

INGREDIENTS

- **12 slices thinly sliced Genoa or similar salami**

1. Place the slices on a hot dry skillet (the salami
   will release enough fat for light panfrying).

2. Flip and fry the salami until both sides get crispy.
   They will puff up a little as they cook, but just
   gently push the puff down when you flip to
   allow for even crisping (that puff can be filled
   with Fromage Facile, page 43, or other mild
   cheese soon enough!).

3. Remove the slices and blot on paper towels. Your
   meat crackers are ready for serving!

OTHER SUGGESTED MEATS

Of course all manner of charcuterie is great on
a cheese platter just as is, no crisping required.
For other meaty cracker options however, bake
or fry bacon, pancetta, and even prosciutto in
bite-size pieces with similar results.

GARLIC AND RAINBOW PEPPER OLIVE OIL CRISPBREAD

SERVES: 4

Cheese counters offer all sorts of fresh and
crispy breads, but a last-minute homemade option
is always good.

INGREDIENTS

- **1 fresh clove garlic**
- **4 flour tortillas, the thicker the better**
- **Extra-virgin olive oil**
- **Sea salt**
- **Coarsely ground rainbow pepper**

1. Preheat the oven to 350°F.

2. Slice the garlic clove in half and rub the halves
   on the whole uncooked tortillas to infuse them
   with flavor. Brush the tortillas with olive oil on
   both sides and sprinkle with salt and pepper.

3. Bake the tortillas in a single layer on cookie sheets
   for 15 minutes, flipping them halfway through, or
   until crispy and slightly brown. When crisp, sprinkle
   with more sea salt if needed, and allow to cool
   without stacking (we don't want them to steam).

4. Serve whole or crack each sheet into rustic
   pieces. The peppery crunch pairs nicely with a
   flavorful cheese like Chivo Fresco (page 75) and
   mild Meyer Lemon Ricotta, too (page 35).

OTHER SUGGESTED CRISPBREADS

Baguettes, lavash, naan, and corn tortillas all
make awesome crispbreads. (You can also fry
them in a pan; use duck fat for an especially
decadent flavor!) Sprinkle with caraway seeds,
citrus zest, fresh herbs, infused salts, or even
spices like nutmeg and cinnamon.

CHÈVRE
FRENCH KISSES
(page 49)

SOUR CHERRY, THYME,
AND HAZELNUT PASTE
(page 226)

SPICY FIGS
IN RED WINE
(page 224)

SPANISH OLIVE AND
TOMATO TAPENADE
(page 228)

Drunken Fruit: Recipe and Formula

You have probably noticed that jewel-hued jars are king these days. Jams, compotes, fruit spreads and pastes are abundant, and can be as exciting as the cheeses themselves. With these formulas, you can make a variety of sweet and savory accompaniments yourself. Enjoy cherries, plums, peaches, pears, apples, grapes, and whatever else strikes your fancy. Changing up the booze and add-ins makes for endless combinations.

SPICY FIGS IN RED WINE

SERVES: 4

INGREDIENTS

- 2 tablespoons honey
- ½ cup red wine of choice
- 4 fresh figs
- ¼ teaspoon ground cinnamon
- ¼ teaspoon ground cloves
- ¼ teaspoon ground ginger
- ¼ teaspoon ground anise seeds

1. Whisk the honey with the wine in a small sauce pot.

2. Slice the figs into quarters and place them in a deep bowl.

3. Add the spices to the figs and toss thoroughly.

4. Add the figs to the wine and simmer on medium for 10 minutes.

5. Spoon the figs out of the wine sauce and serve with Brown Butter Burrata (page 171) or Chèvre French Kisses (page 49). For an extra treat, drizzle some wine sauce over the cheese.

NOTE: If you have extra figs, store them in the wine sauce in a glass jar in the fridge until you're ready to use them. Refrigerated, they will keep for months—as long as they are submerged in wine—getting more infused as they soak.

OR, YOU CAN GIVE THEM AS A GIFT!

DRUNKEN FRUIT FORMULA

You can't go wrong mixing and matching fresh fruit and booze. Work through the formula below with any ingredients you have on hand, and after one round, you'll be ready to go rogue. Each time with the formula should inspire even more combinations. Just go easy on the hard liquor, since only a splash is needed (in comparison to wine). Make adjustments as necessary: If your fruit is tart or not overtly sweet, add the honey, and if your fruit is very delicate, simmer minimally. Otherwise go nuts and keep in mind, the remaining booze and juice is a treat in itself (a warm, mulled cordial!).

Pick one or two fruits ("base"), one booze ("sidekick"), and as many "punches" as you can handle. Follow the steps in the recipe at left to start.

BASE
(1 to 2 cups)

(plus a tablespoon of honey or comparable sweetener if the fruit is not so sweet)

fresh figs, white or yellow peaches, apricots, plums, pears, grapes, cherries, strawberries, raspberries, blackberries, blueberries, persimmons

SIDEKICK
(Splash to ½ cup)

orange liqueur (or any other!), limoncello, rum, brandy, whiskey (just a splash!), red wine, white wine

PUNCH
(¼ teaspoon)

fresh mint or basil, ground or whole cinnamon, cloves, ginger, anise seeds, fresh or candied citrus peel, fresh or candied ginger, balsamic vinegar, pepper

Dry Fruit and Nut Paste: Recipe and Formula

Fig and nut "cakes" are a favorite at specialty grocers. They are packaged in a pressed wedge, round, or loaf, and are most often sliced and presented on cheese platters. Beyond the classic fig loaf, there are lots of variations that can be made using apricots, pineapple, and even humble apples. Use the recipe and formula here to make your own versions to delight your taste buds.

SOUR CHERRY, THYME, AND HAZELNUT PASTE

SERVES: 4

INGREDIENTS

- **1 cup dried sour cherries (or any dried cherries)**
- **½ cup dried apples**
- **¼ cup roasted hazelnuts**
- **½ teaspoon fresh thyme, minced**
- **Pinch of sea salt**

1. Soak the dried fruit in 1 cup of very hot water for 5 minutes to soften it just a bit. Then drain and blot the fruit well.

2. Put the fruit and other ingredients into a mini food processor, if you have one, and pulse a few times for a coarse but evenly mixed texture. Alternatively, chop everything with a knife. Chop roughly but enough so that the apple pieces are no bigger than your pinkie's fingernail (this is flexible; make them bigger if you like the rustic look and bite).

3. The mixture should be able to hold together if squeezed after chopping (add more soaked fruit if necessary). Place the mixture onto a piece of waxed or parchment paper and gather the edges to create a small bundle.

4. Twist the ends of the paper until you have a tight ball. Press in all directions so the fruit and nuts compress tightly, then press down on a flat surface to create a wheel shape.

5. Unwrap the wheel, and it's ready for you to chow down. (It even looks nice right on the waxed or parchment paper!) For platter-worthy slices or wedges, let it firm up in the fridge until fully cool (30 minutes minimum).

FRUIT AND NUT PASTE FORMULA

The most important thing is to keep the ratio of
your base fruit higher than the nuts or seeds so
that it can all compress well together.

TIP! Quickly toast the nuts and seeds on a dry skillet while your fruit soaks—the flavor will come alive!

**Pick one or two ingredients from each column and follow the steps in the recipe on the facing page.
The ratios are starting points—use what you love.**

BASE
(1 to 2 cups)

raisins (golden and regular),
dried cherries, blueberries,
persimmons, mango,
apricots, prunes, figs, apples,
pears, pineapple, banana

SIDEKICK
(½ cup)

shelled and roasted
hazelnuts, walnuts,
cashews, pistachios,
almonds, Brazil or
macadamia nuts, pecans,
sunflower seeds, pumpkin
seeds

PUNCH
(½ teaspoon)

fresh mint, thyme or
rosemary, anise, caraway
seeds, dried peppercorns or
sea salt, citrus peel, ginger,
cacao nibs

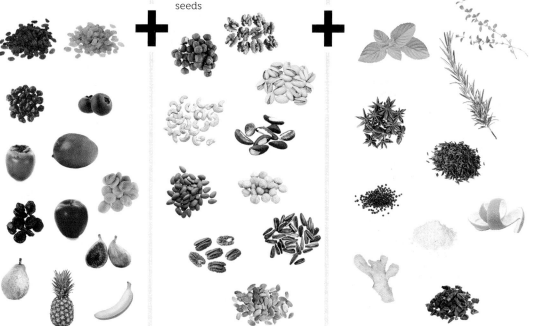

Tapenade: Recipe and Formula

A tapenade is salty and tangy, chunky but spreadable and, like many favorite condiments (pesto, salsa, and so on), it can be mixed in endless varieties. It turns the ordinary into something rich and satisfying (and not just in the cheese world—baked potatoes, fish, and sandwiches are *all* better with tapenade). Traditionally from the French Mediterranean, tapenade is salty and oily and usually contains capers and olives—though it certainly does not have to. Its flexibility lies in its taking on anything from mushrooms to anchovies, accepting what seasonal bounty is available, and stretching ingredients into something magical.

SPANISH OLIVE AND TOMATO TAPENADE

SERVES: 4

Spread your tapenade on crostini and eat it with a mild cheese that will balance the saltiness—perhaps Fromage Facile (page 43) to keep with the French theme?

INGREDIENTS

- 1 cup green Spanish olives, pitted
- ¼ cup paste tomatoes, diced (canned are okay)
- 1 small clove garlic
- Zest of 1 organic lemon
- ½ teaspoon fresh oregano
- Sea salt to taste
- Lemon juice, optional
- Olive oil, optional

1. Put all ingredients (except the lemon juice and olive oil) into a mini food processor, if you have one, and pulse a few times for a coarse but evenly mixed texture. Alternatively, finely chop everything with a knife, or coarsely crush it in a mortar and pestle (and really feel the Mediterranean tradition!).

2. Adjust the salt and add a squeeze of lemon juice or splash of olive oil if you'd like more moisture. Mix it up.

TAPENADE FORMULA

Create your own signature tapenade by keeping a good balance of salty, crunchy, spreadable, and tangy; taste as you go and you'll do great! Loosely follow the ratios suggested, but let your taste buds be your guide. (Note: All of the base ingredients are available canned or in jars. Of course, if you grow veggies and can your own tomatoes, peppers, and eggplant, this is a great way to use them!)

Pick two or three from each column and follow the steps in the recipe on the facing page.

BASE
(1 to 2 cups)

pitted Kalamata olives, pitted Spanish green olives (stuffed are fine), pitted black olives, marinated artichokes, roasted sweet peppers, marinated mushrooms, roasted eggplant, grilled or roasted asparagus

SIDEKICK
(¼ cup)

capers, cornichons, pickles, sauerkraut or kimchi, sun-dried tomatoes in oil, diced tomatoes (fresh or canned)

PUNCH
(½ teaspoon)

fresh rosemary, thyme, oregano, mint, dill, citrus juice, olive oil, citrus zest, fresh/roasted garlic, anchovies, basil pesto

MIX IT UP: No-Fail Formula for DIY Cocktails and Mocktails

With this flexible DIY mixology formula, you can pair any leftover herbs from your cheesemaking escapades with bar staples and, using these tips, be ready to offer someone a drink 1950s-style in minutes. Beyond this recipe, use the formula to experiment with ingredients (it's curious; creativity really flies after the first cocktail). Amidst all the ensuing merriment, make sure to note which combos you like for next time!

Cocktail

Feel free to change up the herbs or the citrus or adjust the sweetness. This flexible recipe makes a refreshing herb-infused lemonade with a variety of fresh ingredients to complement your cheeses; try sage, thyme, mint, or even cilantro!

HERBAL GIN AND SODA
MAKES 1 COCKTAIL; SERVES 1

INGREDIENTS

- 2 sprigs rosemary, divided
- 1 sprig lavender
- ½ organic lemon cut into 2 wedges, or 2 tablespoons of lemon juice
- 2 tablespoons agave or simple syrup
- 2 ounces gin
- Splash of club soda

1. Use a wooden spoon's handle to crush one sprig of rosemary, the lavender, and the two lemon wedges in a shaker or tall glass.

2. Add syrup and gin, then shake or stir fiercely.

3. Strain into a short wide glass filled with ice, and top off with club soda.

4. Garnish with the second rosemary sprig and sip or serve.

VARIATIONS + SUBSTITUTIONS

- Use ⅓ cup green grapes with 2 sprigs fresh mint and 1 sprig thyme and leave out the lemon and syrup. Garnish with a grape.

- Feeling dehydrated today? Replace the gin with more club soda or sparkling water and make it a mocktail!

- See the formula for more!

BASIL
FAUX-JITO
(page 232)

CURRIED
PANEER
(page 67)

HERBAL
GIN AND SODA
(page 230)

Mocktail

BASIL FAUX-JITO

MAKES 1 MOCKTAIL; SERVES 1

Mint is not the only refreshing herb suited for cocktail hour. Basil's crisp flavor makes this blended mocktail every bit as special and thirst-quenching as its inspiration libation.

INGREDIENTS

- 5 leaves of fresh basil, plus 1 leaf for garnish, or 2 frozen basil cubes (see box, below)
- 1 cup (8 ounces) sparkling water
- ½ cup ice cubes
- 2 tablespoons agave syrup or simple syrup, or 2 large medjool dates, soaked and pitted
- 3 tablespoons lime juice
- 1 slice of lime, for garnish

1. Place 5 of the basil leaves, the sparkling water, the ice cubes, the syrup or dates, and the lime juice in a blender and blend on the highest speed until slushy.

2. Pour into a tall skinny glass or Mason jar and garnish with the basil leaf and the lime slice.

3. Serve chilled, with a straw.

VARIATIONS + SUBSTITUTIONS

- Use kumquat juice instead of the lime juice and replace the sparkling water with coconut water. Garnish with a kumquat.

- Do you like the sound of this but just seem to think something is missing? Go on, add a splash of rum! (Or any other liquor from the Formula chart, opposite.)

- See the formula for more!

CAN'T USE THE HERBS RIGHT AWAY? MAKE HERBAL (OR FRUITY) ICE CUBES!

If you don't have a green thumb or you just find yourself with too many herbs at some point, making herbal ice cubes is an easy way to have that fresh flavor available later. Blend herbs like basil, mint, lemon balm, or lavender with just enough water to allow blending and freeze them in ice cube trays. Once frozen, pop them out and store in freezer bags to keep them fresh-tasting for at least a month. Fruit can be mashed up and frozen without water; store it in the same way. The herbs or fruit may darken a little but the flavor will be there. Substitute basil ice cubes in the blended recipe above or just use as pretty and flavorful ice cubes to cool plain water.

COCKTAIL/MOCKTAIL FORMULA

Since your friends will be begging to toast your amazing feats of curd, you might want to provide them with a refreshing glass to raise at your next cheese party. This chart can be the starting grounds for myriad concoctions—whether boozy or not.

Insert some ingredients from the lists below into the cocktail and mocktail recipes that I've given you, or really get inspired and devise your own creations using the ratios.

Choose a couple from each section and play. Use desserts, international cuisine, seasons, or cocktails you have had as inspiration.

BASE
(2 ounces hard liquor, 6 ounces wine and not-booze)

Wine—your choice: sparkling wine, champagne, vodka, gin, rum, whiskey, tequila, sparkling water, club soda, coconut water, kombucha

+

SIDEKICK
(1 or 2 splashes, to taste)

Infusions (DIY is fun!); bitters/tinctures, cordials, liqueurs; shrubs or drinking vinegars; citrus, fruit, and tomato juices; strong brewed tea (decaf or herbal mint, green, Earl Grey, jasmine, Darjeeling)

+

PUNCH
(1 to 3, start slow and add to taste)

Fresh herbs (mint, basil, sage, thyme, rosemary, lavender, lemon balm, cilantro); citrus peel; ginger; rose or orange blossom water; fresh or frozen fruit (berries, grapes, melons!); pickles; cucumbers; fresh chili peppers; spices; salts

Chapter 5

BONUS DIY DAIRY ESSENTIALS

THREE NONCHEESE RECIPES FOR DIY DAIRY LOVERS

After all we've been through together, I would regret it terribly if I didn't teach you to make some old-fashioned dairy basics! Butter and ghee both fit within our one-hour theme, but yogurt and yogurt cream cheese are level two as far as wait time is concerned. Luckily, they could not be any easier, and once you see how simple it is to make all of these favorites, you will be glad to have the skills under your belt.

Butter

MAKES: ABOUT 8 OUNCES

There are very few things as delicious as the butter you will make yourself. It's worth every minute of the twenty that you'll need to invest.

INGREDIENTS

- 1 pint (2 cups) cream (store-bought heavy whipping cream or skimmed from unhomogenized milk)
- 3 to 4 cups very cold water
- Salt to taste, optional

SUPPLIES

- Food processor or mixer
- Wooden spatula
- Glass jar with lid
- Small funnel
- Large mixing bowl
- Medium bowl (for water collection when you "wash" the butter), optional
- Crock (for storage), optional

NOTE: Butter made from grass-fed cow's milk will take on a deeper yellow color than conventional butter because of the beta-carotene in grass.

1 Pour the cream into the food processor and close the lid.

4 Continue on high until the bits become a single large chunk of butter. It should take less than 8 minutes. At first, you will see and hear splashing, then you may hear a thud and see a ball of soft butter appear suddenly.

2 Start the machine on low, then quickly go up to medium, then crank it up to high (this is just to prevent a lot of splashing).

3 After about 5 minutes, look for separation: Fat (butter) separates from the liquid (buttermilk) and yellow bits of butter will begin to form.

5 Use the spatula to hold the butter as you pour the liquid—real buttermilk—into a jar (use a funnel if necessary). Cover the jar and refrigerate it so you can make buttermilk biscuits or pancakes later.

6 Move the butter into the large bowl (larger than seems necessary) so you can wash and press it.

7 Pour a cup of very cold water over the butter and use the wooden spatula to mash it, thereby "washing" it.

8 Hold the butter back again as you pour this watered-down buttermilk into a medium bowl, if you plan to use it (you can cook rice in it, use it in a cream soup, or use it instead of water for biscuits), or pour it into your sink.

11 Pat the butter with a clean paper towel if you still see beads of water. Place your butter in a pretty crock for storage or right onto your baked potato!

NOTE: Fold finely minced fresh herbs like parsley and chives into your soft butter, and enjoy it on anything from cucumber sandwiches to scrambled eggs.

9 Repeat steps 7 and 8 several times until the water runs clear (this process helps preserve the butter longer). Then add salt to taste or skip to step 11 if you choose to make unsalted butter.

10 Squeeze the butter a bit more since the salt will draw just a bit more moisture out.

SHAKE IT BUT DON'T BREAK IT (AKA THE JAR METHOD)

If you don't have access to a food processor or electric mixer, pour the cream into a jar with a tight lid, and then shake the heck out of it. It works. I have actually done this at a dinner party. I baked bread for everyone, and then we passed the jar around. The person who is shaking it when the cream separates is the winner!

Even if you have a food processor, it's worth trying the jar method at least once because you can actually feel the change in your hands when the butter appears. Wash, drain, and salt the butter, following steps 6–11. (Pro form: Use two hands!)

Whichever method you choose, in the end, you will have real buttermilk and butter. (Real buttermilk will not be thick or cultured like what you see in grocery stores now, which is cultured low-fat milk). It is more watery and not tangy—but it is a delicious mild alternative to use in any recipe that calls for buttermilk.

Ghee (Clarified Butter)

MAKES: JUST UNDER 8 OUNCES

The advantage to ghee is that you get the taste of butter minus the smoke if you try to fry with it. Ghee offers the best of both worlds *and* it can be left at room temperature without spoiling. It makes a perfect fat to use for our Plantain and Cracked Pepper Crackers (page 220) or Butternut and Chive Crostini (page 221). It also happens to be the primary fat used in Indian cooking, so if you ever decide to make a curry from scratch, it's important to have ghee on hand. Additionally, you can use it just like butter on waffles or when making cookies.

INGREDIENTS

- 1 cup cold butter (or more, if desired)

SUPPLIES

- 2-quart stockpot
- Large mixing spoon
- Metal sieve
- Coffee filters or butter muslin
- Glass jar with lid

1 Place the cold butter in the pot and bring it to a simmer, then to a boil, over medium heat. This will take about 5 minutes for cold butter. Look for white solids swirling around in golden fat.

4 When the top is less foamy, you may see that the creamy milk solids have sunk to the bottom of the pot. It's okay if the solids get a little toasted but the ghee will have a more neutral flavor if they remain lighter in color. Do not stir at this point.

2 Reduce the heat to the lowest setting as soon as you see the butter boil and foam.

3 The foam should dissipate as the butter continues to simmer and turns just a bit golden, about 2 minutes.

5 Turn off the heat when you see little to no foam and can clearly see that the solids have separated from the golden liquid. Allow the ghee to cool for 20 minutes.

6 Line the sieve with coffee filters or butter muslin.

7 Pour the ghee into the sieve, straining it into the jar.

8 Remove the solids-filled filter and sieve, leaving behind the ghee in the jar.

9 Your ghee is ready to use! Cover with a lid when completely cool, and store at room temperature. (Ghee may also be stored in the fridge if you would like it to stay firm.)

TIP! The toasty, salty solids that are left over are not wasted in India. Try putting them on rice or bread—yummy!

Low-Tech Yogurt

MAKES: 1 QUART

What's tangy and delicious, easy to make, and has been around longer than cheese? Yep, that's right: Contrary to popular belief, you don't need a yogurt maker to make yogurt. Just gather a few common items you have around the house, along with some active culture yogurt as a starter, and you can make yogurt perfection, filled with beneficial bacteria. From there, you can make sweet or savory dips, Greek-style yogurt, and even cream cheese! (Or just add sea salt—it's incredibly refreshing!) Note, though, that homemade yogurt does not contain additives like gums and gelatins—so it will not be as thick as the store-bought variety, but you can drain it a bit at the end to thicken it.

PREP: To avoid contamination while you ferment the milk, rinse everything that will come in contact with the milk in boiling water. (Note: It should go without saying, but do not eat any batches that smell bad or look moldy!)

INGREDIENTS

- 1 quart milk (4 cups; whole cow's milk will produce a richer yogurt, while goat and low-fat will produce a less rich, loose yogurt)
- ¼ cup live culture plain yogurt (any fat content)
- Fresh fruit, preserves, honey, or maple syrup to taste, optional

SUPPLIES

- 1-quart stockpot
- Cooking thermometer
- Large mixing spoon
- Large pot, optional
- Large whisk
- ¼ cup
- Choice of fermentation method setup (see page 246)
  a. Insulated quart-size Thermos
  b. Insulated picnic cooler and two quart-size glass canning jars with lids
  c. Quart-size glass canning jar in oven with oven light

1 Pour the milk into the stockpot and bring it to a simmer (185°F to 195°F). Stay close, and watch the pot to make sure that it doesn't boil over. Stir the milk occasionally to prevent a skin from forming on the surface.

2 Turn off the heat, and quickly cool the milk to 110°F by placing it in a sink or larger pot of very cold water.

3 Thoroughly whisk the ¼ cup of plain yogurt into the cooled milk until it is fully dissolved. This is your starter.

6 Stir the cool yogurt in order to develop a smoother consistency. (And remember, homemade yogurt will not be as thick as commercially made yogurt because it doesn't contain additives or thickeners.)

7 Enjoy your yogurt plain or mix in fresh fruit, preserves, honey, or maple syrup to taste. Alternatively, add nuts, seeds, or herbs and salt for a savory treat.

NOTE: Save ¼ cup of your plain yogurt as a starter for the next batch.

4 Immediately pour the prepared milk into the Thermos or canning jar, seal, and allow the milk to culture for the necessary time required by your chosen fermentation method (page 246). In all cases, more time means more tart flavor.

5 The yogurt will be warm and very loose after fermentation. Refrigerate for at least 2 hours to fully set the fermented yogurt and allow it to thicken and develop flavor. (It is worth the wait! Warm, soupy yogurt is an acquired taste.)

YOGURT TROUBLESHOOTING

Surprising results? Keep in mind that most yogurt fermentation problems have to do with maintaining the warm temperature for enough time, but here are a few common issues unraveled.

- Does your concoction look thick like yogurt, but doesn't taste tangy? Ferment it a bit longer in a warm place, checking every 4 hours.

- If your cultured milk cooled too quickly, warm the milk back up to 110°F (no hotter or you will kill the cultures!) and return to step 4.

- What if the yogurt tastes tart, but is liquid-y? Try adding more time to the fermentation process as well as the cooling/setting period, if needed. Check after 4 hours of either.

- See a big separation between yogurt and whey? Mix or drain it and make a note to cut the time in the future. (This separation will not harm anything—you still made great yogurt!)

- If nothing happens after 24 hours, discard your batch and start over. Your bacteria may be too weak or old.

FERMENTATION METHOD SPECIFICS

Slow is the way to go when it comes to DIY yogurt. The longer you ferment, the tangier the yogurt will be, and the more probiotic activity it will have, but 24 hours is a good cutoff when using any of the methods explained here. On the flip side, if your impatience is getting the better of you, you may use a clean spoon to taste your yogurt as soon as you see that the milk has thickened (which can happen as early as 6 hours after fermentation has begun, depending on warmth and time of year); if it's not tart enough for your taste buds yet, allow it to ferment longer.

THERMOS

CANNING JAR

a. Insulated Quart-Size Thermos Pour the warm cultured milk (110°F) into the Thermos and seal it tightly with the lid. Allow the milk to ferment for 12 hours (or until the desired flavor and texture are reached).

b. Insulated Picnic Cooler and Two Quart-Size Glass Canning Jars Fill one jar with water heated to 185°F, and seal it tightly with a lid. Pour the warm cultured milk (110°F) into the other jar, and seal it tightly with the lid. Place both jars in the cooler. Close the cooler lid, and allow the milk to ferment in this warm environment for 24 hours (or until the desired flavor and texture are reached; try the taste test described above).

c. Quart-Size Glass Canning Jar in Oven with Oven Light Preheat the oven to 200°F for 5 minutes before turning it off. Pour the cultured milk into the jar and seal it tightly with the lid. Turn on the oven light and place the jar in the warm (but turned off!) oven as close to the light as possible. Close the oven door, and allow the milk to ferment for 24 hours (or until the desired flavor and texture are reached).

WANT TO MAKE THICK YOGURT OR YOGURT CREAM CHEESE?

To thicken your yogurt, use some of your nifty cheesecloth to line a small colander with a bowl underneath. (Sound familiar?) Add the yogurt and allow it to drain at room temperature until you like the consistency of the yogurt: You can achieve Greek-style yogurt in 4 hours, cream cheese in 12 hours, and the Mediterranean cheese called labneh in 24 to 48 hours if you add salt (2 teaspoons per pint) before draining.

appendix

RESOURCES, READING, MY THANKS, AND MORE

SUPPLIES

Find every cheesemaking supply and any equipment called for in the recipes at these establishments. I am a bit shy to include my own site here, but I do sell the supplies that will make things fail-safe for you.

urbancheesecraft.com (that's me!)
DIY Cheese Kits, vegetarian rennet tablets, citric acid, salt, molds, cheesecloth, advice

culturesforhealth.com
Calcium chloride and other fermenting supplies (for cultured dairy, pickles, sauerkraut, etc.)

williams-sonoma.com
Urban Cheesecraft Kits as well as pots, colanders, spoons, thermometers, measuring cups

etsy.com
Handcrafted cheese platters, serving dishes, cutting boards, knives, little bowls, cute things

thegrommet.com
Condiments, crackers, nuts, chocolates, honey

mountainroseherbs.com
All-natural organic spices, blends, dried herbs, edible flowers, culinary salts

atthemeadow.com
Specialty salts, peppercorns, bitters, chocolates

amazon.com
All of the above and everything in between

FURTHER READING

For additional reading, check out these tomes that I like to keep in my cheesemaking library. They're listed in order of difficulty level—from easiest to most challenging—so you can supplement your cheese education at any point in the process.

Home Dairy, by Ashley English (Lark Crafts, 2011)

The Cheesemaker's Apprentice, by Sasha Davies with David Bleckmann (Quarry, 2012)

Artisan Cheesemaking at Home, by Mary Karlin (Ten Speed Press, 2011)

Home Cheesemaking, by Ricki Carroll (Storey, 1982, 1996, 2002)

Mastering Artisan Cheesemaking, by Gianaclis Caldwell (Chelsea Green, 2012)

COMMON CONVERSIONS

LIQUID		
2 tbs	1 fl oz	30 ml
3 tbs	1½ fl oz	45 ml
¼ cup	2 fl oz	60 ml
⅓ cup	2½ fl oz	75 ml
⅓ cup + 1 tbsp	3 fl oz	90 ml
⅓ cup + 2 tbsp	3½ fl oz	100 ml
½ cup	4 fl oz	125 ml
⅔ cup	5 fl oz	150 ml
¾ cup	6 fl oz	175 ml
¾ cup + 2 tbsp	7 fl oz	200 ml
1 cup	8 fl oz	250 ml
1¼ cups	10 fl oz	300 ml
1⅓ cups	11 fl oz	325 ml
1½ cups	12 fl oz	350 ml
1⅔ cups	13 fl oz	375 ml
1¾ cups	14 fl oz	400 ml
1¾ cups + 2 tbsp	15 fl oz	450 ml
2 cups (1 pint)	16 fl oz	500 ml
2½ cups	20 fl oz	600 ml
3¾ cups	1½ pints	900 ml
4 cups (1 quart)	1¾ pints	1 liter
6 cups (1½ quarts)	3 pints	1.4 liters
8 cups (2 quarts)	4 pints	1.8 liters
4 quarts (1 gallon)	8 pints	3.8 liters
2 gallons	8 quarts (16 pints)	7.6 liters

TEMPERATURE*	
90°F	32.2°C
95°F	35°C
100°F	37.8°C
105°F	40.6°C
110°F	43.3°C
115°F	46.1°C
120°F	48.9°C
125°F	51.7°C
130°F	54.4°C
135°F	57.2°C
140°F	60°C
145°F	62.8°C
150°F	65.6°C
155°F	68.3°C
160°F	71.1°C
165°F	73.9°C
170°F	76.7°C
175°F	79.4°C
180°F	82.2°C
185°F	85°C
190°F	87.8°C
195°F	90.6°C
200°F	93.3°C
205°F	96.1°C

WEIGHT	
½ lb	227 g
¾ lb	340 g
1 lb	454 g
1¼ lb	567 g
1½ lb	680 g
1¾ lb	794 g
2 lbs	907 g

* To convert °F to °C:
Subtract 32, then multiply by 5, then divide by 9.

To convert °C to °F:
Multiply by 9, then divide by 5, then add 32.

ACKNOWLEDGMENTS

I am a huge fan of both cookbooks and craft books. I have always appreciated the work that clearly goes into them, and I respect the authors immensely, but I never, ever imagined they were such a collaborative labor of love until going through the experience of publishing one myself.

So many people helped me complete this book, it's ridiculous. (DIY, my bootie!)

First and foremost to thank is Jeff: I have no words, honey. I love you. How did I get so lucky to have someone encourage me and up my game at the same time? Thank you for having dinner with me at three a.m., for making my spaghetti arms look semi-normal in the photos, and for washing piles and piles of dishes. (Okay, I had a few words after all . . .)

To my mom, Lupe, who instilled in me both a healthy appetite and a can-do spirit. Thank you, Mom. I hope you consider my work your achievements, too—because they are.

Friends and family, too many to name, thank you for asking for constant updates on the book (with proud twinkles in your eyes). Your enthusiasm for tasting and testing my creations warmed my heart again and again. I hope every one of you shares some piece of yourselves with the world; I am so grateful

you share yourselves with me. A special shout-out to Tami Parr who generously shared a book proposal of hers with me (so I could know what one looks like!) and encouraged me to believe I, too, could do this—thank you!

Colleen Waldref, thank you for holding down the cheesy fort while I wrote, tested, and rewrote. I could not have left everyday business to a better VP of Sales and Operations!

Huge thanks to all of my DIY Cheese Kit customers, retail and wholesale. I would not be writing a book at all if you were not interested in making cheese at home—but your support is so much more than that. Your sweet emails and photos of your lovely cheeses make my work meaningful.

I want to thank Debbie Stoller for being an early fan of my DIY Cheese Kits and an inspiring business mentor, and for sending Workman and my editor, Megan, my way. You may have a future in matchmaking, Debbie!

I could not have conjured a more collaborative, talented, and pleasant publishing company to work with than Workman Publishing. As it turns out, books are not just written by the author—so much

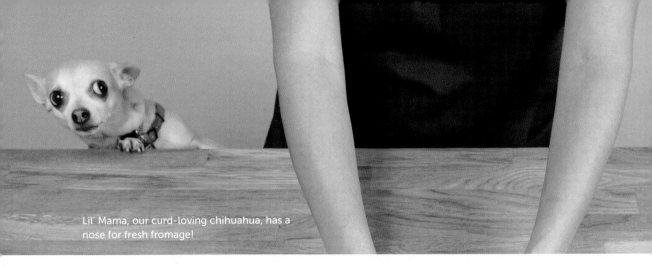

Lil' Mama, our curd-loving chihuahua, has a nose for fresh fromage!

more is crafted by a skilled team. I mean, how cute is this book?

Megan Nicolay, my editor, I thank my lucky stars almost daily that you are who you are. Working with you has been a true, uncomplicated pleasure. And Liz Davis, your work is not overlooked—thank you for your kind words and keen eye.

Anne Kerman, your encouraging photography tips and sense of humor made a huge difference in the scary beginning.

Sarah Smith, your early interest in making cheese as well as your commitment to getting a feel for my DIY Cheese Kit design came through in the fun and details of the book's look. Thank you for caring enough to make the book complement my style.

I could not possibly forget Lil' Mama, our curd-loving Chihuahua. Mama, you are always up for anything, whether it's staying up with me while I make cheese at one a.m.

(yeah, I know it's because you want some, but it still counts) or taking cuddle breaks in the sunshine when I've been at the computer too long. Thank you, sweet girl.

See? I am so, so lucky. Go, team!

AND THANK YOU, READER! IF YOU WERE NOT AN INTERESTED, CRAFTY, FOOD-LOVING DIY ADVENTURER, THIS BOOK WOULD NOT HAVE A PURPOSE. THANK YOU FOR SHARING IN MY LOVE OF FRESH CHEESE AND FOR SUPPORTING MY WORK!

Claudia

INDEX

H

Haloumi:
    in grilled eggplant rolls, 101
    recipe for, 93–100
Hand shaping cheese:
    bocconcini, 192–94
    classic party log, 188–89
    cutting, 186–87
    firm curd, 184–87
    molding, 184–85
    petite bonbons, 190
    pinwheels, 195–96
    pulled curd, 192–98
    ravioli, 197–98
    soft curd, 188–90
    wrapped cheese, 199–200
Hazelnut, sour cherry, and thyme paste, 226
Heat, for cheesemaking, 18
Herbal gin and soda, 230
Herbs:
    dried, embellishing cheese with, 208–9
    dried, keeping on hand, 14
    dried, layering into cheese, 210–11
    fresh, buying, 14
    infusing cheese with, 204–5
    making herbal ice cubes with, 232
    whole, embellishing cheese with, 206–7
    see also Basil; Rosemary
Holy cannoli dip, 41
Honeyed toast cheese:
    recipe for, 83–90
    in strawberry-covered chocolate
        cheesecake, 91

I

Ice baths, 19, 148–49
Ice cubes, herbal, creating, 232

Ingredients:
    acids, 12–13
    herbs and spices, 14
    milk, 14–17
    rennet, 17–18
    salts, 18

J

Jicama crisps, 218

K

Kebab party, 143
Kitchen prep:
    cleanliness, 7
    equipment list, 7–11
    maintaining equipment, 11

L

Lemon, meyer, ricotta:
    in holy cannoli dip, 41
    recipe for, 35–40
Lettuce:
    grilled cheese sammies, 111
    wraps, curry in a hurry, 73
Lime:
    -chipotle Oaxaca, in cucumber ribbon
        salad, 169
    -chipotle Oaxaca, recipe for, 161–68
    juice, note about, 71
Low-tech yogurt, 243–45

M

Measuring cups and spoons, 10
Mediterranean olives, 217
Melty and gooey cheese:
    brown butter burrata, 171–81